Lives of the Soul

2010 Frederick E. Dodson

Table of Contents

1 Viewpoints of a Soul

2 The Souls Amnesia

3 Astral vs. Celestial

4 Death and Transition

5 Soulmates and Soul-Guides

6 Mission of the Soul

7 Choosing your Incarnation

8 Lucid Dreaming

9 Awareness

10 How to Access Future Lives

11 Soul Awakening Exercise

1

The Viewpoint of a Soul

Not much is taught about the life of the *real you* that resides in a broader non-physical perspective. This is because the soul intentionally came here with amnesia. To reveal the life of the soul is a little like cheating. But alas...we must at least reveal this much, because humanity has been taking the game of life just a bit too seriously. The *you* we are talking about, sees the "big picture"; it has the overview over "past" lives, "future" lives and more importantly, the *Lives between Lives*. What happens *between* incarnations is actually more interesting that what happens in "past lives". From our earthly perspective we imagine the plane from which the soul comes to incarnate on the physical plane as an "etheric" or "subtle" plane that is on a "higher level" to which we can "ascend". In my experience these esoteric and spiritual teachings are analogies and not totally accurate. It seems as if earthlings are taught this stuff in words that a mind can grasp. Sometimes the mind is taught fairy tales, auxiliary metaphors that could otherwise not be understood on mediocre levels of consciousness. My descriptions of the souls planes that follow will also be mere metaphors and analogies that are less than accurate. But I intend to make them at least more up-to-date and a bit more precise than the watered-down descriptions we are told so that we can "digest" them. This is the year 2011 and we can handle a little more depth and accuracy, right?

The non-physical reality is not just a "higher level" or "other level" but the physical world is actually *enclosed* in it. The model I use is that of many concentric circles – universes within universes – with the physical world being the smallest one included in all of the bigger circles. This is the exact opposite of what contemporary science teaches...that consciousness is included "within" the material world. This would also mean that the world, the whole material universe, is included *within* Consciousness. This is important because it changes your perspective from "here is tiny wee me in a grand and huge universe" to its reverse. Another model that works would be looking at the outermost tiny edge of a long stick. You have this long stick that includes all-that-is...and on the very tip of it, as a little "extension" so to speak, you have the entire physical universe. If we therefore place too much importance on the physical world, the outer world, the material objects, we are ignoring 99.99% of all-that-is. This is not to promote escapist or ascensionist fantasies – since we deliberately chose to be here, now at this physical place – but to widen our sense of perspective.

Neither is the non-physical plane as "vague" and "subtle" as we imagine it to be. On many levels it is less vague than our three-dimensional world. In these realms it is more intense, vivid and elated than our world.

Including concepts and worlds beyond your 5-senses, beyond your earthly existence (without assigning too much importance to them!) will increase your enjoyment of earth. As the relative importance of daily events decreases because you know "there are other things out there", your enjoyment of those daily events may also increase because you are no longer solely dependent on them.

2

The Souls Amnesia

When on the non-physical plane, the soul chooses a planet to incarnate on. If it incarnates into a physical dimension, it also agrees to *forget* everything other than that. Why? So that it can "play the game" without prejudice and baggage from all other Lives. It can participate in the game of life with a fresh zest for things...as if seeing them for the *first time*, from a completely blank slate. Amnesia of all other planes and realities allows you to focus exclusively on to the physical dimension. If it were not for this amnesia you couldn't focus properly. That would be like trying to play chess while there are all kinds of noises and other things going on around you. Or like playing chess without rules and limitations where you just wipe the opponents pieces off with one brush of the hand. But if you had that power...it wouldn't be a game, would it? Neither would it be enjoyable or something you could learn from.

Since you are in fact reading these lines, that's an indication that your soul permits a bit more leeway and a bit less suffering. The reason many don't want to read or know this is because it would disturb their act, their party, their task and mission on this planet and they'd have to incarnate *again* in order to fulfil their plan. But then there are souls who needn't come back again and have allowed themselves to find out more.

So where did I pick up the information on the *Life of the Soul*? I picked it up in Meditation. Proper Meditation allows me to access Information unfiltered by the world-mind or Ego. Letting go of thinking you have to or even can know everything else opens higher channels of knowledge. I have also witnessed and experienced much of what I am talking about in this book through lucid dreaming and out-of-body travel.

In the last three decades other Researchers have been able to make enormous progress in fishing for data from non-physical realms. This began with a kind of advanced Hypnotherapy that was not only able to regress to childhood and achieve stunning feats of healing and realization but allowed a person to regress to the times before childhood...into past lives...and more importantly...*the lives between lives.* The first evolutionary step in Hypnotherapy (which is a quite different art from contemporary hypnosis) went beyond normal "Regressive Therapy" and discovered not only a dozen or a hundred past lives of the soul, but many thousands. The next evolutionary step was called "progression hypnosis" and began with the realization that one could also access *future lives,* or more precisely *"future probability lines"* to some extent. Finally, the most advanced form entered our collective knowledge with the introduction of regression/progression to lives between lives. What happens between the incarnations of a soul? What happens after the body dies? Up to that point we'd only heard of "near death experiences" (NDE) and what happened in the vicinity of death. Our knowledge of what happened beyond that was fuzzy...because we rarely have people come back from long-time death to tell the story. What happens before the soul is born into a world again? The Evidence for the accuracy of accounts gleaned through advanced hypnotherapy lies in the consensus of many different accounts made by many different therapists and many different patients from many different backgrounds and cultures. These accounts also happen to roughly agree with channelled information about the non-physical realm and they also happen to agree with my own experiences. This depth of *congruency* between the varying accounts and case-studies and the usefulness and effectiveness of much of the information gained does suffice to make fairly precise statements about the nature of the realms beyond...without the need to trust in watered-down ancient scripture.

Channelling has also made leaps in the last decades. Channelling is the process of a medium letting herself fall into trance or increasing her *vibration* and receiving communication from a being residing the purely non-physical or semi-non-physical. This is more of a "reception" of telepathic signals and feelings rather than an entity taking control of the person. These energy-pulses are translated by the channel into words...messages from beyond. At the turn of the last century, channelling was often a matter of communicating with ghosts and the deceased. It was more of a spiritualistic practice than a spiritual practice. Nowadays, a different quality of channelling is arising. The sources channelled are no longer those of the astral-plane or the spirits of the deceased but indeed higher-vibration beings of angelic levels, higher-selves and beings with quite a different message than those known in centuries passed. Much of the "reality creation materials" are semi-channelled. In the end it is effectiveness and usefulness of the information that is more important than the specific source.

The information received in the last decades is both confirmed by and at odds with ancient scripture. The Biblical and Hindu concepts of Heaven and Hell, describe, to some extent, what can happen after death on the non-physical plane. But the Christian description is misunderstood in many ways. "Eternal" suffering is something that does not exist as the non-physical definition of time does not include the concept of "forever" in the sense of an unlimited amount of *time*. Neither is the non-physical limited to two locations called "heaven and hell" but to *trillions of different worlds* and variations. The Hindu and Buddhist ideas of "reincarnation" also touch upon a half-truth, on something the soul experiences to some extent. However, contrary to far-eastern doctrine, reincarnation is *not mandatory*, much less reincarnation back to earth and even less into "plants and rocks". There are trillions of worlds out there and religions have a tendency to limit the amount of experience a soul can make. Such limitations do not really exist. It is also a falsehood that we "must" incarnate in order to work off our Karma. A soul can choose not to incarnate at all but hang out on soul planes for the entirety of its existence. It will not experience the benefits of incarnation in that way, but if it chooses to remain non-incarnate, it can do so.

Within my own travels to the soul plane during meditation, lucid dreaming and out-of-body-experience I could find confirmation for some of the conditions described by others. What I can say for sure is that there are *regulated sequences* a soul goes through, independent of one's belief-system. Existence has an *order* and a *meaning*. For the philosopher, the intellectual and the enlightenment-teachers this is important to know. If you experience this first-hand you discard Nihilism, Fatalism, ideas of meaninglessness, coincidence, chaos and you understand that there is a point to life. Life is worthwhile.

In learning about the non-physical you first collect information on an intellectual level, think about it, consider it. Most of this will be completely new to you. Some of it is meant to inspire memory and break through the amnesia just a little bit. Once you start extrapolating from the data given you know your mind as grasped the basics.

But that's not enough. The soul is not primarily interested in information but in *experience*. An experience of the non-physical is achieved by inner journeys (meditation, lucid dreaming, OBE) and by communication with your "soul-guide" or higher self. You might also want to find out a little more about your "general mission" or "life's purpose" that you intended before you came here. The key question you can ask yourself concerning this is:

"Is there any information about me that I might not be aware of?"

3

Astral vs. Celestial

An altered state of Consciousness is not necessarily a Higher State of Consciousness. Spiritual Adventurers frequently mistake the two. They think that because they are feeling or seeing or hearing differently than ever before in their life, that they are in a "Higher" State of Consciousness. But on a felt Frequency-range of Energy, there are different levels of Consciousness, as I describe in my book "Levels of Energy" So if you are, for example into taking hard Drugs, you can easily experience altered states of consciousness – but they are not "higher" states at all. With hard drugs you will go astral, see spiritual Dimensions, access energy-fields, see entities because the Drug turns off the mind temporarily. And instead of having to Meditate for months and months, you get your glimpse right away. However, what you are seeing on Hallucinogenic Drugs, for example, are lower-astral-planes (as opposed to higher astral planes and celestial planes). That's why the overall effect of these trips on your daily life will not really be positive. You will be experiencing phases of delusional thinking and lethargic inertia. That's why taking mushrooms or similar may be a good idea once or twice, just to get an idea of other Dimensions of Reality, but anything beyond that is detrimental. The other reason I recommend staying away from Drugs is because they condition the mind to believe that altered states are more easily possible with the help of outside substances. This type of dependency only adds to the already existing addictions the Ego has (Food, Drink, Internet, TV, Sex). It only acts as an additional burden. The more spiritually free you become, the less dependencies you should have (this is not to say that spiritually free beings don't have sex or don't watch TV, but to say that they no longer *rely* on these things for happiness).

An altered state is not always a higher state. The visions you can see in Horror films are images from altered states and alternate Dimensions of Reality. But do they look like Higher states to you? Not hardly. They are the stuff of nightmares.

So before you start "contacting entities from the other

side", don't automatically assume that because they are from they other side that they are higher than you. Not all extra-dimensional beings are higher than you. Some only pretend to be. Do a check whether their overall messages allows you to feel more joy, love and strength over time or whether it is detrimental over time.

I knew a girl who started channelling an entity, naively assuming that she is talking to something higher. It turned out that all the entity really wanted was to feed off her energy because it didn't have any of its own. Outsiders saw this because her life deteriorated rapidly in all areas. I also know people who are in "contact" with entities and their lives take a turn for the better. This is simply to say: Do a check of who you contact and why you contact beings from "the other side". If you are coming from lack, you will attract beings who use your lack-energy to peddle their stuff. The "other side" is, in many respects, no different than earth. There are also well-intentioned and not so-well-intentioned over there.

I don't recommend contacting Ghosts and the deceased either. Why? Because these are mostly earthbound spirits who, for some reason, are still attached to earths field.

These are energy-entities that "didn't make it", so to speak. Contacting them is of zero benefit to you (Exception: If you are a professional ghost-releaser who helps earthbound ghosts to free themselves from their attachment and ascend).

When you purchase products that promise you an altered state of consciousness, do a check. Will these products give me an overall Higher State or only an Altered State? If they provide an Altered State you may feel spaced out for several hours...but your life or attitude will not improve. If they provide a Higher State, you may or may not be spaced out, but the effect will be an improvement in your knowledge, strength, joy, attitude or in specific life results.

A rough differentiation of the frequency-ranges and levels one can access is lower-astral, higher-astral and celestial. If you harbor hatred, fear, grief, craving, anger and you use the techniques in this book, you will access the lower-astral realms. If you harbor a normal state or one of neutrality, acceptance, curiosity, interest, general-well-being, you can access the higher-astral through using the techniques in this book. If you are in a state of joy, love, peace, bliss or deep relaxation while using these techniques you have a chance of accessing Celestial realms. Like energy attracts like energy, it's really as simple as that. This is why it is important that at the moment of your death, you are somewhat at peace with yourself and the world.

4

Death and Transition

When we die we are sometimes taken by surprise that we are actually still alive. The more immature or brainwashed the person was during life, the longer and the grander the surprise. Most souls recuperate quickly and the fog of amnesia starts to lift. They remember their life as a soul which is actually their *main life*. They remember that their stay on the planet was actually only a side-life, a temporary experiment, one of many lives. A soul is born and dies many, many times in the course of it's development and exploration.

Consciousness can be seen as three concentric circles. The smallest inner circle represents your mind, your daily focus, your ego. The second circle, which contains the first, is a kind of subconscious or sub-awareness in which all memories and experiences of this and other lives are stored. And the third circle, which contains both of the others, some call "super-consciousness" or higher self. This higher self is your true identity which also contains all of your sub-identities of all lives and the ego-selves of all incarnations. Higher Self is the soul itself and represents the center of our wisdom and a viewpoint beyond life and death. (See my book "Parallel Universes of Self" for more on Higher Self and sub-identities).

After death most people experience themselves floating above their physical body, observing it from outside and "still existing". Since the incarnated earth-ego is conditioned to feel death as something sad and shocking, the soul can often observe how those relatives and friends who were left behind are in grief. For this reason it sometimes attempts to console or positively influence those left behind. Some souls are frustrated over the fact that they cannot touch or communicate with family members and friends (yes, a soul is able to feel frustration). The reason that it is difficult to contact the bereaved and tell them "I still exist! All is well!" is because of a *vibratory mismatch*. Their grief is on a different frequency than the souls relative *elation*. Elation cannot communicate with grief. If the bereaved could just relax a little and remain aware, they'd be able to sense the presence of the soul right there in the room with them. If you ever experience the death of a person live, then try it out. Rather than succumbing to grief and sorrow (you can keep that for later) try to become aware of the soul still hovering in the room or space above. You can sense its presence by a tingle on your skin or an air draft in a room in which the windows are closed. If you are very aware you might hear the souls communication which often manifest as feelings or voices that were not created by your imagination. And in an even more aware and relaxed state you can even see them as a ball or fog of light. A typical place to experience such phenomena is a hospital. This is why a large percentage of "belief in afterlife" and accounts of ghost-sightings come from nurses and doctors. Another way to view afterlife realms to some degree is by staying somewhat aware in a state of half-sleep. It is the state between sleeping and waking that benefits so-called "astral vision". Children are more likely to notice the "presence" in a hospital room because they are, in those moments, not preoccupied with worry.

After the first shock of having died, the soul continues in a more calm and observant mode by moving away from the scenery of the body. Being stripped from the heaviness of body and mind and the conditioning falling away rapidly, any possible shock, frustration or sadness does not last long. Usually within minutes it is replaced with a sense of floating lightness and elation which has no match in earthly experience. This moving away from the body is accompanied by a pull-, or tunnel effect. Even while the soul is still attempting to move or touch objects or communicate with the family this *suction* commences. The effect hardly ever causes worry or doubt but is instead accompanied by feelings of deep peace and ease and, a bit later on, gentle euphoria and brightness. An uneasy feeling is only experienced with those souls who have identified with earthly reality to the extreme or have resided on a low level of energy. These rare cases cannot take the sudden shift from low to high and go through a process of healing and integration (which we will touch on later). Almost all accounts describe a *brightness that does not seem to have any specific source.* This is as if the "air" itself is charged with light. Despite the suction-pull which would seem to let people think they are other-determined by some outside force, most feel a sense of unlimited freedom. Some souls experience the suction as a trip through a tunnel at the end of which an even brighter light awaits them. Near-Death-Accounts usually get this far in their description.

Although the soul can wear many masks and make itself look differently, in it's normal state it looks like an egg-of-light a luminous ball. In a way, every soul is its own star, its own source of energy. You are, quite literally, a star! "Normal" souls are perceived in the colors white and white-yellow. Other types of souls are perceived in other colors. The experience of leaving the body often feels like the peeling of a banana. Despite initial disorientation and possible trauma caused by violent deaths the sense of peeling off the body is felt as relieving, freeing and even humorous. The soul floats in an "air space" that is no "air space", a weightless, gravity-less, limitless environment. Initially this "space" will feature some of the environment of earth or the room in which the soul died (The soul allows itself to slowly get used to the planes environment right after death), but as time progresses, this familiar environment is gradually replaced with the limitless expanse which is neither pitch-black nor light but a sort of "mix". Imagine an expanse all around you, to every side and horizon that is "dark" but charged with light-particles. Although you can control your movements here, the pull nevertheless guides you to journey-points which every recently deceased person passes through. The pull is like a calling and is accurately described in most Movies and Books on the subject. The direction in which the pull guides the soul *is* brighter and lighter, which already here, indicates differences in energy intensity. There are a few rare souls that are not quite ready to leave the place of death or earthly sphere just yet and through their free will are able to withstand the pull for awhile to extend their time in earths atmosphere.

Contrary to popular myth, most souls are not interested in what happens to their bodies after death. Only some decide to hang around "a few more days", spend time near family members and friends or visiting places they lived until the funeral is over with. On this non-physical plane there is a sort of "time" but this time is sped up so that the days that pass up to the funeral are like a few hours to the soul. The pull of mysterious origin is appealing and feels good which is why most souls are not eager to hang around earth any longer but to move with it. Motivations for still remaining on earth at this point, vary. Those who have experienced an extremely violent death tend to linger around earth longer because they are actually still upset or resentful. Resentment creates an energy-field that gives you some Heaviness as not to ascend. Just like a diver will put on weights as not to resurface, a soul sometimes puts on negative Emotions as not to resurface to his true self. Also those people who die an early age tend not to want to let go of earth immediately, as if there were some unfinished business. Abrupt death is a shock especially to souls less experienced. But even these souls almost all leave after only a few days (for those who hope to sense the presence of their deceased loved ones: Don't count on it after a weeks time.). Some do like to show their appreciation for those involved in the funeral procedures. The few that don't leave after this time are the "lost souls" or "earthbound souls". These are what our culture terms "ghosts" or "haunting ghosts". Those waiting for contact from the "deceased" wouldn't really want to get in touch with any soul that is still lingering after weeks. These "disturbed souls" that do not follow the light away from earth do so because of some unsolved issues that had extreme impact on their consciousness. In most cases it is not the actual "souls" that have stayed behind, but *split-off* parts of the soul, "shadows of one's former self". There is a "squad" of soul guides and helpers assigned to help with the "integration" of these split souls. Where is the other part of the split soul if not on earths sphere? It is aimlessly wandering around somewhere on the dreamlike astral plane. The old 90s movie "What dreams may come" gives some accurate descriptions of low and high planes and what happens to lost souls. A haunting

Ghost may be able to hide from these soul guides for some time, but eventually all souls return to the light-space that serves as a transfer-point from earth-sphere to the original realm of souls. Having an earthbound entity haunting a house for "hundreds of years" is only a few weeks for the astral plane and only a few days on the soul plane. Most of the "haunting" in various Houses as portrayed in movies and literature is exaggerated. These "Apparitions" are often not the core soul itself but split-off energy phenomena or "entities" that keep repeating the same program. Nevertheless, these entities suffer and require some kind of loving attention and care. More of a problem are split-off energies and entities that stick to human energy-fields. These need to be freed by Emotional Clearing and raising your own Vibration.

Except in tragic cases involving very-low-energies (see my book "Levels of Energy), the suffering of a split-soul never takes that long. The soul-transfer-system works in perfect order and can only be averted temporarily (by the souls misguided will). Well...yes, it is technically possible for the soul to never follow regular procedure and resist the suction and transfer...if that soul so decides. The free will of a soul is inviolable. But this is a more rare event than Horror-Movies or Religious Fire- and Brimstone

Preachers try to make us think. "Horror movies" of earth serve the purpose to instill fear of the non-physical in the youth as to strengthen the amnesia and unawareness of the soul plane and to draw people into the belief in lower-astral planes. Once you learn that you cannot experience any reality you do not vibrate in sync with through your emotions and beliefs, Horror movies become hilarious nonsense.

One purpose of sharing this data with you is so that conditioned aspects of your consciousness can mentally prepare for the "death" event. Learning this will make the process even more smooth than it already is. With your attention somewhat freed, there will be certain stages after your death that you do not have to go through. The quickened pace of proceedings will allow you to take care of other, higher things. Truly, the transit from earth to the soul plane is only a small step compared to more important subjects that await the soul. Smooth and quick death proceedings might even spare you the necessity to reincarnate on earth again. Of course, if you behave suspiciously or like a complete beginner at the "border checkpoint" (threshold), they might send you back! (Just kidding...or am I?). When death nears anyone can blend his consciousness with super consciousness. Dying is much easier for the soul than living on this planet. It's like taking a *hugely rewarding break* from a tough sports match. This is why we can often detect a rather smug facial expression on the faces of those who have died. The peaceful expression indicates that this person has blended with higher self. It's funny in a way: We associate death with "loosing life energy" when in fact the opposite is the case. By dying you *regain* all your energy. But mind you, this is not an invitation to suicide. Suicide is a surefire way to become a problematic earthbound-soul. Rather than "solving" an issue suicide prolongs an issue by transferring it to the non-physical realm.

Dying is not really dying anyway. It's more like ceasing to look through a magnifying glass. You've been focused on earth all your life, and then you quit focusing on earth as your prime preoccupation. Therefore dying may feel just as odd as anytime on earth you leave something you have been highly involved in. If you have ever left a long-time relationship or a job you have been in for decades, then you know what Death can also feel like (apart from the Elation you get through being free from the body). If you have had such events in your life you are actually vibrating closer to the soul-plane in those days than in other times throughout your life. If you have difficulty letting go you suffer over no longer having that job or partner or house or whatever you are leaving behind. But if you left voluntarily or are good at letting go, then going into the new, going into the great unknown, causes you to feel high, adventurous, elated.

And indeed you can "practice Death" by going into the Unknown in Life. The easier it is for you to do so, the easier death will be. You can see how "mature" a soul is, in a sense, by checking how difficult it is for a person to walk into the woods at night. This exercise would be symbolic of walking into the unknown. I've seen people who absolutely refused to even consider walking up to the edge of the woods in darkness, let alone into the woods. And then there are those whose eyes light up and they eagerly look forward to taking a walk in the woods at night. That is the difference between "young souls" and "old souls". Old souls are those who have experienced the death moment so many times that they are no longer afraid of the Unknown.

The migration to the next level of being is easier than reported on earth. In fact, everything "up there" is easier than reported by the insanely negative earth-mind. First there is a soft pull towards the light which gets brighter as you close in. Often described as a "cloudy brightness" or "shining fog" this is the first "official" place the soul visits after death. Here the soul feels a power, peace and *presence* which is hard to describe in earthly vocabulary. Imagine feelings of empathy and friendship magnified tenfold and you get a sense of this transfer point. There is also the clear sense of "someone waiting for me with open arms". Earth and the physical universe are at this point no longer perceived but still "felt" to some degree. On it's journey to this "reception hall" the energy body still goes through various adjustments and "tunings". The soul is now very well aware that it is not "dead" at all but very much alive and going *home*. Remembrance of "who I am" floods in. Some souls observe their surroundings with utter awe while more experienced souls proceed with acceptance as if following routine-procedures. Some readers will be surprised to learn that there are more and less experienced souls and that even here there is a sort of *evolution* of souls, yes even hierarchy. If you, dear reader, are surprised by this remember the credo *as above so below*. Earth is in many respects a miniature version of the non-physical universe, so there is no reason that the next level should not also have aspects of hierarchy, order and progression. The One, Infinite, Non-

Dual space I and many others refer to as "Cosmic Consciousness" is still way, way, way above this level and not all too relevant to the missions of humans. The realm we are addressing still does have a sort of time, albeit not linear but more like a spiral. In this chapter we are addressing the second and third concentric circles enveloping the small circle of the physical/material, we are not addressing the not the "all-that-is".

There are some very advanced souls that move rapidly through all the *stages*. They hardly notice the grandiosity of it all. These "Pro-Souls" are, at least on earth, in the minority. The average soul is slower, more appreciative of the beauty and sometimes even hesitant. The average soul is often welcomed by friends and relatives (formerly deceased) and a soul-guide and whatnot, while the professional soul speeds straight to their destination (the Home-Universe which matches their energy level). The less experience a soul has with birth, death, re-birth, the more amazement it displays for the afterlife process.

After awhile the light-fog clears and one leaves the tunnel. Many report that at this stage, conditions are still somewhat unclear and unsure. We are still residing on the "astral plane" which is the most dense of all spiritual realms. Advanced souls recognize the space they are now in as *layered*. One can perceive many transparent layers of light, some more expansive, some smaller, some curved, some spiraled, some notched. They do have the relative appearance of solid physical structures although they are not physical in the sense we mean it. The Light strata are inter-weaved and are sometimes described as looking like electrically charged strings. The impression is that of Symmetry with variations in Density and thickness or intensity of color. The layers or strata are in motion. What are we looking at here, though? We are actually looking at different unique spaces within the overall realm we are in, different "worlds" and vibratory experiences/levels. Different places the soul travels to. To get an idea of the limitlessness of it all: The entire physical universe is a tiny speck of dust (remember the concentric circles?) compared to this realm. A good description of this space can be found in the books "Far Journeys" and "Ultimate Journey" by the Astral Traveler Robert A. Monroe.

This layered space is also witnessed when moving back towards incarnation. You can picture the space as one of huge storeys of varying, waved, round and straight light-layers. They curve away from you when you float towards them. They do not curve away from you if your vibratory level matches theirs. Have you ever had a dream in which you were desperately trying to reach a destination but never could quite get there although it seemed very close? This reflects your inability to enter a space which you are not the corresponding energy match to. The colors and lights on your journey to your "home" (vibratory-match field) have an extremely calming and regenerating effect on the soul. The sounds and tones can be roughly compared to bells, cymbals, strings and bowls that vibrate according to your movements in this space. While on earth your body moves according to the sounds (dancing), on this plane sound moves according to *your* moves. Some travel on the resonant frequencies of these sounds like on the waves of a gigantic tuning fork. The beautiful sound vibrations start relatively quickly after your demise from earth as a hum, drone or rush/sweep/white noise and increase after you leave the earth spheres to a universe-filling sound that revitalizes your entire being. It's as if the divine powers have set up the most stunning and beautiful show imaginable for the returning soul. In addition to the play of light carpets, colors and sounds some can spot objects remotely reminiscent of physical objects except in that they display a beauty or size unseen on earth. Diamond-like cities, luminous spheres, cones and other geometric designs, majestic crystal cities, lush fields, mountains and landscape-like spaces, buildings with mind-bogglingly fantastic rooms and furnishings and objects never seen on earth are some of the things described. Some souls temporarily find themselves in odd replicas of places they enjoyed during their incarnation. "Odd" because I suspect these have been put in place for newly arrived souls who have difficulties adapting to the grandeur of the realm. And as fantastic and magnificent and stunning this vast space is, it's not even "the heavenly abodes", it's not even the Celestial Level yet. The higher astral is about 1000 times as beautiful as earth. The celestial is about 1 Million times as beautiful as the higher astral.

The stage after leaving the tunnel is meeting either friends and relatives who you knew during your incarnation (formerly deceased) or soul-friends. Soul-friends (for lack of a better word) are the ones you are familiar with because you were incarnate with them on earth at one point in this life or another life or ones you hang around with on the soul-plane (some of which were never incarnate). After this you usually meet the Soul-Guide. It is common that you enter a "new space" before meeting these beings. On earth spaces are marked by buildings, public places, fields, streets, country-borders. In the afterlife they are marked by changes in energy or visual appearance. On the soul plane its a lot of fun to have different spaces and borders and to cross into them. The chronological order of events does differ from soul to soul. Some do not meet anyone after death but only after arriving to their home-base. Oftentimes you meet your friends while your soul guide stands nearby waiting to "take over" after greetings have been exchanged, other times soul-guide and friends welcome you at the same time. Some are greeted neither by friends nor a soul guide but only by a soul mate. Advanced souls do not require being met by their friends at every single discarnation. This resembles earth behavior: The parents take their young and inexperienced child to school and pick her up. But after she gains some experience and age she is left to go to school and come home by herself. Some very advanced souls are not even met or picked up by their soul guides and instructors because they are soul guides *themselves*.

Your relationship to your soul guide or your own mission as a soul guide (in rare cases, no more than 0.1% of earths population work as Soul Guides of the afterlife) is one of the most important aspects of your overall evolution as a human and a soul. Your *soul guide* is a soul that is on another vibratory level and on another level of development who has been *assigned to* you (by even more divine sources/forces) and with whom you have developed a trusting and fruitful relationship over the Millions of years of incarnation and discarnation. During your incarnation you mostly forget this friendship and guidance (which occurs in addition to the guidance you receive from your higher self during incarnation) but the deep relationship is quickly remembered "on the other side". Your forgetfulness of one of the most important beings in your existence is somewhat of a running joke between you and the soul guide. In fact you are probably reading this right now and doubting such a being even exists. Your doubt in the existence of a relationship spanning millions of years and many universes is the height of ignorance...but you are forgiven :-) While your relationship to soul mates and friends and relatives is somewhat significant, your relationship to your soul guide and to yourself are more important. With the soul guide you elaborate on experiences of your last incarnation and scheme out new learning or experience tasks, games, and experiments for further incarnations on the same planet, other planets or other realms and dimensions. Those souls who have returned from their last incarnation slightly traumatized or exhausted meet their soul guide immediately. These advanced beings are able to take on and transform the souls pain to immediate relief, helping to heal the wounds and regenerate. After that the soul guide conducts an elaborate "coaching". This later stage, which is conducted "at home" includes *evaluating* one's last life. This process has been distorted by biblical ideas of "judgment and punishment of one's sins". But again, this is the view of things filtered through the absurdly negative and silly earth-mind. What is still in effect on soul plane however is the "law of attraction" or "law of correspondence" by which you get back what you radiate out. If for example you have committed murder during your incarnation it is possible that you will have to reincarnate in order to get murdered. Why? In order to balance out your energy fields. Another option is to experience the same in "small doses", not by getting murdered yourself but by a number of smaller pains inflicted on you during incarnation or outside of it. This is perfect justice in action. There is no need for a higher committee to "judge and punish" you because you will necessarily get back what you put out, sooner or later. It is possible to postpone the "getting back" for awhile or to take the hits in small doses, but you cannot avoid it.

Energy naturally stays in balance by getting rid of all excess.

Just to elucidate the difference between what I call Higher Self and Soul Guide: The Higher Self is you. You can either communicate with that Higher aspect of yourself, or, if you are fairly advanced, you can just Be the Higher Self. The Higher Self is the Soul. It is you without the body-mind. It is you as an energy-field that has a broader perspective of several lives and incarnations. The Soul Guide is an even higher being in the grand scheme of things. It is who your Soul addresses for advice and consultation.

Despite the stages you visit after death not being the "total enlightenment" or "the freedom from all suffering forever and ever" hoped for by scholars and mystics of earth, even though it is very euphoric, relieving, loving and refreshing. Even when traveling alone you never feel left behind or isolated. A loving presence permeates the entire realm. The newly arrived do not have too much time to just float around and get a look at things though because they are processed through various stages. For most souls this order of things is very welcome. For some rebellious souls, like myself this sometimes felt like some kind of conspiracy that had a pre-paved way with pre-paved checkpoints that were hard to deviate from. It reminded me of an earthly airport in which the only way you can go is straight and on to the different stations pre-determined by the airport and it's security personell. My soul has occasionally rebelled against "standard procedures", but with experience I began to realize that the suction-pull is leading me to precisely the places that are a match to by vibratory signal...precisely to the places that are right for me, that are my home. And as my vibration is largely self-created the place the suction takes me is ultimately created by me. The Universe is only responding to what I have put out. Sure I could leave the trail but sooner or later I'd have to return to where I belong. And there's not too much to be found off-trail, similar to there not being too much to be found when branching off trail at an airport. Add to that that advanced souls don't even follow the regular proceedings anymore but are led through wonderful lounges, "VIP Doors" and private jets taking them to exhilarating heights. But until then the process is:

1. "Death".
2. Leaving the Body.

3. Being pulled through a Tunnel.
4. Travels through the Soul Realm.
5. Being welcomed by friends and the soul guide.
6. Transit to your Home

Techniques and Meditations

These are some optional contemplations that will assist you in deepening your connection to and memory of the non-physical. Your memory and recognition during this earth life will never be complete, but it is possible to "get back in touch" with to some extent. You can't be entirely disconnected anyway. Source is where you come from and where you will go back to naturally...no matter what you do or don't do. This is the only thing you have no choice or free will over. As to when or how you return to source...that's up to you.

1. The purpose of "negative" experience.

Even if you don't want to hear it, the soul purposefully and intentionally chooses a few "negative" experiences and limitations for its incarnation. Understanding what these are and why they were chosen, will speed up the lesson-learning and spare you more troubles. Why?

Because the pre-chosen "negative" experience only happens *once*, unless you resist it instead of learning from it instead of being someone courageous and shining *in the face of it*. Suppress and badtalk it and it happens again and again and again and again and again, in many variations. Once you recognize the positive *pay-offs* or reasons of the negative event, you can re-decide and re-focus a new *life and timeline*.

a) On a separate piece of paper, write down the three most negative events of your life.

b) Ask yourself to each of these events: What *would I have not learned* or understood without these events?

c) Write down a negative event of which you fear it may yet happen in the future.

d) Ask yourself about each item: What *would I not learn* or understand if I wouldn't make this experience?

e) And now the secret to avoiding this experience: *How can I also learn this lesson without having the negative experience?*

This very evening, before falling asleep, address your soul guide (as a beginner, simply imply that he always listens and hears *everything*) in about the following way:

"I know that it was intended that I have this experience during this lifetime. But I no longer want to make this experience. I can learn the lesson required in a positive way too, by doing the following:
_____ (make your suggestion). Thank you for showing me that this issue is already resolved".

Fall asleep in a feeling of piece and pay particular attention to any dreams you may have during your sleep.

2. Recognizing your partner as a soul mate

Many of the people you meet in your life are "old faces", acquaintances and friends you knew before entering this life, people you agreed to meet before you incarnated. Take some time to look at your spouses or friend from this viewpoint of "having known them for a long time". Act as if you accept this old and secret agreement has been made and that you both know *exactly* what you are doing. You have chosen each other as reflections and go through certain experiences together.

While looking at your partner in this way, thinking about him/her in this way (or maybe even talking about this with him/her) notice the "knowing" response or glow in your partners eyes, even if superficially he/she denies it. This "wink of the eye" over your shared game, that everything was planned out before incarnating will increase over time. Look it your partner with an increased sense of awe...the way you'd be looking at her/him if this were really true (because it really is true). Your relationship will gain a new kind of depth. Getting close to a soul on earth that you have never met before is rare. While it does happen, even those encounters with souls "you've never met" are encounters with souls you will meet in a future afterlife setting. Most people are, under the thin surface of appearances, all too familiar with each other and *only acting* like it's "the first time we meet". After all, it's one of the experiences a soul longs for: Experiencing things for the first time. Hence the self-imposed amnesia. Of course the whole drama of "breaking up" and "loosing a loved one forever" is also only an act, because in infinity, nothing and nobody is ever lost. If you could see that sad drama from a soul plane viewpoint you'd find it hilarious. Of course, when we're in the middle of "loss", it doesn't feel that hilarious.

Nevertheless it is something to consider the next time we think there is a "loss" of someone or something.

3. Memory of Other Lives

If you are one who practices Meditation (and knowing the importance of the inner world compared to the outer world, hopefully you are) you may sporadically include attempts to remember other lives. If you have "flashbacks" or thought-sparks that seem to have no relation to your current life or memory of this life, chances are they originate from other lives. This is not uncommon as your soul has constant access to all lives and planes. Speculate...

What are some ways you might have died?

With what possible deaths could ailments you've had during your life be connected with?

To which culture or place in the world do you feel "strangely" attracted?

Any idea why you might feel attracted to that place or culture?

If not, then there is some information about your relationship to that culture that the memory banks of your mind do not have but your soul does. Extend your attention towards that life and culture in your meditation. Feel it. By being there with your attention you start vibrating the way you did when you had a life at that place.

With a little bit of self-confidence and allowing your attention to wander around to *other things than your habitual thought*, you can actually enjoy some insight into past lives, even future lives and finally life-between-lives yourself. But if you want support from a hypnotherapist, only search out the best after careful examination. Otherwise you will land in the offices of some kook who tells you are the reincarnation of Cleopatra and Elvis Presley. In fact anything the hypnotherapist *tells you to imagine or think* goes beyond the duty of guiding you into a state of trance where these things come up by themselves. A competent hypnotherapist will not attempt to influence the results of your "channelling" while in trance.

I can also recommend my Guided Audio Meditation "Journey to Another Life" for intensifying your awareness of your other incarnations. It is available at www.realitycreation.net.

5. Out-of-Body Travel

The ability to have out-of-body-experiences is actually obstructive (!) to the mission of most souls because it means bypassing the self-imposed amnesia barrier. The desire to ascend to astral realms is then a *contradiction* one's own former decisions. It is possible that you gave yourself some leeway on this subject though. If so, astral travel will usually happen *naturally* without much effort or only a few practice efforts. If it takes an enormous amount of work to get results then it's not really part of your life's plan. A cup of coffee before going to sleep will benefit the little experiment: Lie down and stop moving. Simply stop moving. Your mind is moving but the body is not. Let your body relax, breathe and fall asleep while keeping your mind awake and aware. This might require some type of focusing (on a spot on the wall or an object or a thought). If, due to this practice, your body starts vibrating, your heart-pace quickens or you perceive strange sounds (astral noise), then you have given yourself some leeway or ability to astral travel to certain parts of the non-physical. The next step would be to relax your heart beat and willfully intend to leave your body or float away. Repeating this procedure will, in cases that it is granted by your higher self and soul guide, lead to astral travel. Take note that anything that comes naturally to you, is in alignment with your souls plans. If you'd like assistance with out-of-body travel I recommend my Audio-Meditation-CD entitled "Out of Body Experience" available in the Internet at realitycreation.net

6. Relaxing Down into Delta State

How connected you are to the soul and afterlife realms depends on how relaxed you can allow your body to be. Having a relaxed body and mind leads to feeling more energy and feeling more of your soul. Some measure progressive states of relaxation by the frequency of brainwaves. Traditionally, the scale goes from Beta to Delta.

High Beta

Panic, Tension, Fear, Racing Mind, Short Breathe, Defensive, Contracted

Beta

Normal Waking Life, Awake, Alert, Attention Extroverted, Lots of Thinking, Working, Talking.

High Alpha

Normal Waking Life but Relaxed, Calm, At Ease, Content, Observing, Aware, More Open, At Ease

Alpha

Relaxed, Dozing, Meditating, Attention Introverted, Dozing, Drowsy, Creative Thinking. In this state you are normally on the verge of falling asleep. If you manage to stay awake and aware, interesting things start happening. Stay awake here and you become more perceptive, lucid, your intelligence increases, you can think both more clearly and deeply. Learning Languages is more easy in this state, among many other things.

Theta

For most people this is just sleep. If you manage to stay a little awake and aware here, lucid dreaming becomes possible. If you stay fully alert despite your body being fully at rest, extrasensory perception, high intuition, reprogramming your mind and its beliefs, spontaneous healings and other altered states are possible. Experienced Meditators have no problem staying awake in Theta.

Delta

This is near-death which is why out-of-body-experiences, paranormal perception, time-jumps, the miraculous is more likely to happen. Dimensional Travel and access to Parallel Universes is also somewhat easier from here.

Just in case you were wondering why me and other teachers in the new-age/spirituality field harp on and on about Relaxation, Meditation and Releasing, this is why.

All the special abilities are found in inner Silence and Deep Calm.

Deep Relaxation, Happiness and ability to Concentrate are interrelated. Where only one of these is exercised, all others are too. A good exercise to try out for Deep Relaxation is to stay awake while slipping into slight trance. Depth of Trance and ability to stay awake will vary at different times of the day. "Normal Life" is either getting Tired when relaxing or getting Tense when fully awake. The state of wakefulness combined with Relaxation is the perfect Union. Each of the following Exercises can be tried out for 15 minutes or more.

Exercise 1

Tense the right foot and toes for a few seconds. Relax them. Tense the left foot and toes for a few seconds. Relax them. Proceed like this for each part of the body, including your face.

Exercise 2

Take a soft, gentle and deep breathe in. Hold your breathe for 5-20 seconds (as long as feels comfortable). Breathe out softly and slowly. Repeat this several times.

Exercise 3

Close your eyes and imagine/feel a sense of *falling, letting go, sinking, releasing everything.*

Exercise 4

Lie down and give up all resistance to everything. Unknow everything. Forget everything. Breathe out any tension. Loosen all muscles. Relax deeply and profoundly.

Exercise 5

Get comfortable enough to fall asleep. Get as close to sleep as possible without actually falling asleep. If this seems too difficult for you, then add something uncomfortable (for example an unnatural body position) to your exercise that keeps you from falling asleep. There are many interesting phenomena that can occur on the verge of sleep.

5

Soulmates and Soulguides

When we "come back home" we first meet those who are familiar to us (soul mates, friends, the soul guide). In their most natural form we recognize them as luminous energy shapes. Souls can also wear "masks" or take on traits of humans or other beings. Sometimes they put on "masks" so that you recognize them from earth-life and feel more comfortable. Sometimes they put them on for certain occasions or because they want to represent a certain concept or personality. Sometimes masks are used for play. Masks of Personality are also used in Life on Earth, but people forget that these are masks. They think that the masks are "really me". No matter what "role" a soul is currently playing, the energy-form has a color and this color is indicative of the *experience it has accumulated* within all-that-is. In my experience and observation, the general "ranking" seems to be:

White

Yellow

Blue

Violet

In a transfer-stage from white to yellow a soul may also take on the colors gray and beige. From yellow to blue there might be a stage in which the energy-field is green. The yellow stage may also include red and orange. The progression then goes to light-blue, blue, dark-blue, light-violet, deep dark-violet. From an earth-time perspective this progression can take several Billion years.

To the human mind it may be surprising that there are ranks of higher and lower in spiritual realms and that you will find mature and immature souls here. Contrary to the distorted earth-sphere, Hierarchies and Rank are not a cause of limitation or discrimination. Those are earthly inventions. The colors indicate "accumulated experience" but there are no feelings of inferiority or being "offended" by the soul. Those are only traits of the world-mind.

Soul mates and Soul friends are those you have known for a number of incarnations and discarnations, souls you have stayed in touch with, experienced shared adventures with, while soul guides are of "higher rank". They have also spent a long amount of existence with you but as a mentor and path-pointer. Seeing the soul-plane this way is not a projection of my earth-self, as some argue. Instead, earth is a projection or miniature version of the soul-plane. The organization of society on earth is modeled according to the soul-plane.

It is not uncommon to meet "deceased" relatives after death but then part ways with them when going Home. Why? Because some of these relatives live elsewhere, reside in another vibratory frequency. If your energy-field is no match to theirs it is difficult to stay in long-term connection on the soul-plane. It is not impossible, but its an ordeal. One of the special traits of Planet earth is that anyone can meet anyone else. The physical universe is a place where one level of energy can meet an entirely different level of energy. So you can have the mass-murderer alongside the saint, alongside the lawyer, alongside the bus driver, alongside the scientist, alongside the football player. This is possible because Earth vibrates much slower so the mismatch is not felt as unpleasant for awhile. Do you know the saying "Fish and new come guests smell in three days"? It takes about 3 days of earth time to notice a mismatch in energy-fields. On Earth you can either then leave the scene, or ask the other to go, or shift your own vibration to adapt. Which option you choose, depends on how much you are able to take and what your preferences are. On the soul-plane the mismatch is felt immediately and only fairly strong souls are able to stay in foreign realities for a longer period of time. This is because strong souls inhabit a viewpoint above the two respective energy-fields. Seen from a Level 7, one can easily move between 4 and 2. The Level 4 however, having less energy, will have a more difficult time with Level 2.

So if your friend or relatives Energy-Frequency is significantly higher or lower, he will welcome you, maybe hug you and exchange a few words and then leave again for "some other time". There are, however, also many relatives/friends which you will continue to see when home. You will recognize some souls as friends that have taken on many different roles in your lives. "Right...that's David, my husband in the life before my last and my wife in the life before the life before my last!" That's a soul mate...someone you have shared many variations with, and not necessarily only romantic one's...he could have been your enemy last time. It is quite probable that your greatest adversaries are actually your soulmates. I know that's not necessarily something you want to hear, but it's true.

Even if it sounds corny: Our "welcoming committee" is convened beforehand. Nothing in the stages after death is unforeseen or chaotic. Oftentimes a soul that is especially important to you will stand in front of the group of other friends and relatives. It is the re-cognition of long forgotten people that is an exhilarating and reassuring experience in a vast, mysterious and infinite universe. Without the bond of appreciation between its beings, this universe would be strange indeed. In fact, the stages after death are so full of "Aha's" and feelings of intense euphoria, that it makes the entire life-amnesia before that worthwhile. The more of the amnesia is peeled off, the more blissfully radiant the soul becomes. This however, would not have been the case if that amnesia had never been imposed. So here you have one of the main purposes of this soul-shell-game called *life*.

The welcoming warmth and joy received on this plane baffles all description. Compared to it all the tombs of scripture, philosophy, "knowledge" about it are meaningless. An analogy: Imagine a two-dimensional coin – the mere picture of a coin on a piece of paper. You can stack up and accumulate as many of these 2-D paper coins as you want...you will *never*

get a real, three-dimensional coin. The three-dimensional experience and all the knowledge and intellectualizing in the world will never come close to the four-dimensional radiance and energy of this plane. This is why, in practicing spirituality, it is imperative to go beyond mere knowledge into *Experience*.

What's more: You are meeting former parents, children, grandparents, business partners, friends, foes...but without their earthly limitations, without their masks of social reservation an fake politeness. And as such they welcome you in ecstatic joy of *your return* home. And this is a true joy to see you, a true care for you as opposed to the self-centeredness of the incarnate soul. You are back from a long and tiring trip and suddenly there is a cosmic party to your honour Back on earth they are in mourning and sorrow over your death and on this side they are celebrating it. This is a valuable moment, no matter how often it is experienced.

From an earthly perspective these stages on the soul plane are "heaven". But from a more expanded perspective, this is not "heaven" or even "the highest possible universe" but simply a standardized program within the game of incarnation, reincarnation and discarnation. There are other realms and other games being played above and beyond.

After the "party" is over, most of our initial meetings are with the soul guide and these are deeper and more contemplative. You will recognize him/her immediately and also remember all prior meetings with him/her. The Amnesia you had during your lifetime is stable but it is not unbreakable. This is why you'll probably spend some time in wonderment over how you could have ever forgotten the relationship. Most soul guides have names that sound strange or cant even be spoken or remembered in earthly ears (If I tell you an "angelic" word chances are you won't remember it 20 seconds later). Some soul guides do have earthly names they "borrowed" from one of their own incarnations. On earth the Soul-Guide is described in different ways. Some say "Guardian Angel". Others say "Inner Mentor". The Soul-Guide is not to be confused with entities that pose as a Soul-Guide. How can you tell the difference? The Soul-Guide usually communicates through Intuition and in a non-intrusive manner during your lifetime. It would not be channelled or cause extraordinary states of being "spaced out" or even make itself seen. If it does come any closer throughout life, then the experience is so profound and warm-hearted that its unmistakable Astral-Tricksters are more gimmicky and cheap than that. Soul-Guides are essentially androgynous but tend to take on either male or female identities over certain phases of time. This is an analogy of how "time" works on this specific plane:

5 soul minutes = 1 physical earth week

20 soul minutes = 1 physical earth month

4 soul hours = 1 physical earth year

2 soul days = 10 physical earth years

20 soul days = 100 physical earth years

This is a rough analogy only. An entire life of the body/mind feels to the soul like only a month has passed, as if it only went for "extended vacation". From this you can glean that the soul might not place as much *importance* on your "huge life events" as the mind does. Your pain of loosing a loved one may take weeks, but for the soul it only takes half an hour. The more subtle/non-physical/non-dense the realm, the more expanded time is in relation to the physical world. Divine spaces feel one Billion years as one second. Beyond that, any concept of time dissolves entirely. People that overcome grief more quickly are people who are "less dense". The are not like the ice that represents matter but more like the melted ice of water that represents mind or steam that represents spirit. The purpose of spiritual training is to become less dense during this life time. This makes it unnecessary to reincarnate again and again because you have "brought heaven to earth". It is not your job to make Heaven on Earth for others, however, but only for yourself. This is one of the key misunderstandings of some religious folks. Don't try to change others, change yourself!

While incarnate it's difficult to recognize soulmates. This is a purposeful part of the game of life. It can happen through signals, symbols or objects that you agreed upon previously. By "previously" I mean in a discarnate state. It can also happen through the eyes. You look someone in the eyes and notice "something" but can't quite express or grasp *what* you notice. "Hmm...there's *something* about this person" says the mind. The soul knows that you know this person but the body/mind doesn't. When meeting a soul mate on earth you notice that something is familiar when looking at them. You try to remember what, but as the memory banks of your mind do not contain that information, you don't know *what* is familiar. This effect is sometimes surprising, sometimes spooky, sometimes inspiring. Believe it or not, there are souls that – despite instruction on the soul plane, despite preparation of obvious signals, *miss* their soul mate on earth or do not meet their most important "soul dates". Now the world-self will go "Oh my God! That is soooo sad! I missed my very own soul mate!". But that's the world-mind speaking it's usual bland cries of self-pity, not the soul who is a bit more humorous and relaxed about it and will relate funny stories about the "near miss" back on soul-plane. The soul guide likes to tease souls that were too blind to notice their pre-arranged dates. And he/she is right in teasing you because a soul mate is usually shoved in your face in various situations. One of my own experiences of stupidity and blindness was a certain person I kept encountering at *the most improbable locations around the globe.* And we kept saying: "Wow! It's you again! Unbelievable! What a coincidence! Small world!"...and then went our merry way. I've not met the person again because I had already been given 3 chances, but had we pursued it, it might have turned out that we have fantastic business opportunities or something else in common. It is only while writing this that I recognize the blind idiocy my mind dwelt concerning this. It is statistically a near impossibility to meet the same stranger at three different places around the globe. But my mind behaved as if it were just a coincidence and was shy of implying more toward a "complete stranger". Next time I meet the person I'll say "We need to talk!" (Meanwhile I have recognized *other* soul mates, fortunately).

Communication with other souls is on a pure thought-form basis. While it is easy to communicate over "large distances" (from realm to realm for example) it is the easiest when two souls are near each other so that their energy-fields overlap and this "touch" can transfer pulsed-frequencies. Souls are able to block their telepathic (or more precisely tel-empathic) communication so that others can't see it. It is much more difficult to hide information and keep secrets on the soul level but not impossible. To hide information from the soul guide is even more energy-consuming because it is your soul guides job to have intimate knowledge of your lifetime and how you attempt to hide information. So keeping secrets toward the soul guide makes little sense...especially considering that he/she is so close to you that this would be like keeping secrets from yourself (which is something you actually do during your earth-time and thereby create a "subconscious" in which all kinds of things are hidden away). One reason people do not want to raise their vibratory frequency during their lifetime is because this makes everything hidden to be revealed. It's as if the raise in vibration makes a light shine into a dark cellar. This light not only illuminates everything but also warms up that which was frozen. The light of awareness will eventually make all things hidden in dark corners burn away, but you can see from this why many of us actually resist high-energy experience or to ascend too quickly. If the level of vibration is "too high" for you, you will get a heart-attack, not find enlightenment. To get a picture of this: Imagine a flying craft from outer-space accidentally landing in the garden of an old country-woman who has never even seen the nearest city in her life. Do you think she'd be blissed out? Probably not. She'd probably be scared to death. *Afraid of the light.*

The way the soul takes on human traits is in a type of thought-forming process which morphs them into existence. This process shapes a kind of "clothing" over the energy body that is perceived as a certain appearance by others. But no matter how many different faces a soul displays for entertainment, playful deception (of immature souls) or for your comfort, you can recognize a soul by the energy-signal which is *unique* to it. The masks and identities you will mostly witness are human in nature, but every once in awhile you may come across characters alien to you…identities souls have borrowed from *other planets* than earth. If you thought earth is the only place to incarnate to, you are mistaken. Just like you are not the center of the world, the earth is not the center of the Universe. Only humanity, in their endless self-importance think that the earth is above the rest. The earth is somewhat unique, but it is not the only place that these types of lives are played out either. If souls keep choosing earth as a Destination for Incarnation that is because they are romantically attached to it, have become habituated to it. For some, earth is an addiction and they resist the planet changing. If things get too good and easy on earth, it will no longer serve as a Training Grounds for the soul and those souls will then have to go elsewhere. Therefore, the "lets make the world a better place" crowd is not necessarily as smart as everyone thinks they are.

On this level of existence you are not infallible. You are not "God" as some teach. You are an individual and unique energy-being. You have *divine potential*, you are a "viewpoint of God" a "split off piece of all-that-is" and in a certain odd holographic way you *do* have the same abilities as the "Supreme Being", but at the same time you are not impeccable or all-seeing neither all-powerful. I understand how contradictory this must sound, but for the time being there's limits to what the mind, in it's dual way of thinking can grasp. It resorts to calling these concepts "paradoxical". For now we can say you are the Supreme Being and you are also separate from the Supreme Being. The Creator is the Creator and the Creation. The Supreme Being is everything, therefore it is also you. At the same time, the *part* of the supreme being that makes you a unique individual soul is not the same thing as that Supreme Being. Nevertheless you have a more expanded sense of knowledge, potential and power on this soul-level. Your thought manifests more quickly. But still there are higher levels *as which* you could exist. The souls of this plane are in a sort of trainings-cycle. The trainings-cycle is a collection of a few trillion souls that have "separated" from all-that-is a bit (without being really separate). This is one of many, many games in many different Dimensions and Universes. Incarnation to earth is like another separation...a separation of the separated so to speak. You go from 5-Dimensional-Reality into 4-Dimensional Reality. And then you incarnate from their into 3-Dimensional-Reality which is the Physical Universe.

Some souls, before reaching their final stop on the soul-plane, make an intermediate stop

in an energy-pool where they regenerate, re-charge and heal. I guess this would be the soul-planes equivalent of a spa. When passing this area on my travels I can clearly perceive pools of energy and also, quite literally, showers of energy pouring over a soul. I assume that our earthly showers try to imitate the experience. It takes some time for the soul to re-orient and re-adapt to the soul plane.

The earthly mirror of this is jet-lag. Although space and time do not have the same quality as on earth, they still exist as spaces, sections and stations that are discernible from each other. Some souls use this spa-like station to recover from wounds inflicted upon the energy body during their stay on earth. Despite the happy elation of leaving a body, it is not uncommon for a soul to be exhausted after a lifetime on earth. Similarly, when you return from a Battlefield on earth, you would probably prefer to go freshen up and relax for a few days before going home to see your family. The spa-like-space re-instates the souls fullness and potential. All the while, the "magnetic pull" is still calling you Home. The pulling-energy is designed and ordained by the next higher Dimension. The regenerative area is experienced by private, closed-off from the vast space one was previously traveling through. The "intense energy field" of that space recedes a bit, just like a spa dims the lights in certain areas for more privacy and comfort. I do not recall the showers personally although I have seen them. People describe them as warm rays, liquid energy, splashes of bliss, a flow that cleanses ones entire being. Physical lives leave imprints in the energy body. The most intense experiences of each life remain stored, even if some of them abate after awhile. Mediocre memories and emotions experienced throughout life are not stored easily but instead tend to disappear after awhile. Indeed, only the intense and heartfelt earthly experiences are of lasting value. One reason advanced souls don't actually want to "erase" any their memories is because they contain vibrational-information that would be *useful* for experimentation in other dimensions. Access to all memories would mean that these can be re-activated when needed in other planes and on other planets. The experience you are having today in your earth life, even if it is mediocre, may be of use in a place and at a time far, far away. The more immature the soul, the more damaged he/she returns from her incarnation and the more time spent under the "shower". Mature souls on the other hand sometimes don't have any of it removed at all, but instead "integrate it" into their overall energy field. But if there are some energy-pockets that are not entirely washed off there is the possibility of re-experiencing some of the tendencies of that energy in a future incarnation.

The cleansing is usually a prelude to intense "talks" with the Soul-Guide. These talks revolve around examining the last life. In examining the last life further soul rehabilitation and releasing-of-the-lifetime is experienced. During these talks the Soul Guide is humorous, loving and very inquisitive about various details of ones life. The Soul Guide knows most everything about you. It knows your learning habits, weaknesses, strengths, worries, aversions, attachments, joys, desires and goals. The Soul Guide is willing to work with you through various events of your life as long as you are interested. If you do not show interest of your own will, things remain static and unmoving. The Soul Guide will almost never push in any direction. The main discussion point of the talk-session is

"What did you intend prior to your last incarnation and which of those intentions were actually fulfilled and which were missed?"

Intentions you did not fulfil are not "punished" as they too contain valuable experiences as "alternative life paths" that demonstrate your ability to re-decide and exercise your free will to go against what was originally intended. And these too are good lessons. Advanced souls talk sessions tend to be more easy-going and shorter. In general *anyone* who has incarnated has *fulfilled the overall purpose* of their incarnation. Therefore even "failed" incarnations are not really failed but a huge step in progress for the soul. But in a few specifics there are some learning tasks the soul chooses and agrees on for an incarnation and these were either fulfilled or not. One example of a typical learning lesson or life-game is "changing roles". If you spent one life mistreating others it can happen that you spend your next life being mistreated. But for readers of books like this it is not quite as probable that your current incarnation is about suffering. If it were, you would not gravitate toward books such as this one. Suffering is a learning tool of the human who believes that suffering means progress or change, "no pain, no gain". But the more advanced the soul the less this is seen as necessary for progress. But even if you are one of those advanced souls you will not be able to completely circumvent suffering because this planet is based on the *contrast* of negative and positive. It is by cultivating your emotional guidance system and going in directions that feel good for you (rather than following artificial goals) that your suffering will be significantly shorter than that of the overall population.

Most important in all of this is to realize that the soul *likes* to incarnate. We hear a lot of claims of "I don't belong here", "I never want to come back again" and all that. But after you leave here, you will (once again) see things differently from "up there". Suddenly your antagonism towards earth turns into a *romantic memory*. You look down at earth and think: "Well, it wasn't that bad after all, It was quite interesting. Maybe I'll go back someday". The earth game does offer unique experiences some of which are not available *anywhere* else. One of the challenges is to be thrown into some of the most dire or dull circumstances under total amnesia and then rise above them in training your ability to focus on creating better. Some souls incarnate again and again until they have finally "mastered the game". It truly is a game, each incarnation being "another round" and can be repeated until one is in command of it. It actually would be possible to have our "heaven on earth", the full bandwidth of awareness without any suffering or powerlessness whatsoever. But you will not find many souls who *really* want that and are therefore able to have that (anything you are "unable" to do you actually do not *want* to do). The individuals on this planet that are in this peculiar state of enlightenment are no more than a hundred (at a population of 6 Billion). These individuals are experiencing the non-physical and the physical plane *at the same time*, which is an entirely different experience still than one of the two by themselves. Connecting "Heaven and Earth" is one of the most advanced variations that can be played in this overall game. From this it should be obvious that no soul *must* incarnate but that it's a personal choice to come here. While no soul is afraid of incarnation but rather enthusiastic, it is aware of the challenges involved. This is why some souls choose to go elsewhere or to remain on soul plane for a few thousand years before "playing another round". What kind of other planets are these? Refer to quality science-fiction novels to get an idea of that. "Science-fiction" novels are actually "channelled" information. *Imagination* itself is the channelling of ideas through filters from beyond earth. In this sense there is no such thing as "fiction" but only probable-for-you and improbable for you. I do not discern between "truth" and "fiction" but between what is manifest on earth and what is not. As far as I am concerned, everything that you can imagine that exists, does exist in one form or another. In other words, you cannot imagine something that has no existence in Infinity.

Techniques and Meditations

These are some contemplative exercises you can try out to deepen your understanding or intuition of what we've talked about. If you feel like "aw, what the heck, it's all nonsense" during any of these musings, remember that's the amnesia-block in full-effect.

1. When soul mates meet

a) Make a list of people that were or are or seemed important in your life (this may also include some you don't know well)

b) Starting with the first person on the list, remember *the very first meeting* with that person. As you remember: What do you feel? What do you see in the persons eyes? Is light reflecting somewhere? What do you smell? What *symbols* do you see around you and the person or in the background surroundings? Is there something in the surroundings or about the nearby objects that you notice now but did not notice back then? Which colors and shapes are there? Is there any deja-vu sensation with this person? Repeat this type of contemplation with every person on the list. If you discover anything unusual or have feelings of recognition or excitement, make note of that beside the name.

3. Questions to yourself

Try sincerely thinking about these questions and find your own answers to them. If you are going to do this in a quick and half-conscious way, don't do it at all. If you're going to do it, then spend some time contemplating each question.

Is there information about myself that I may not be aware of?

What might my life's intention have been before incarnating?

What things in life interest me the most?

What do I want to explore?

Am I fooling myself by acting like I don't remember the life of my soul?

How can I increase my feeling of appreciation towards this life? (Appreciation frees you from the necessity to reincarnate again for the same lessons)

3. Intensifying Appreciation

Appreciation is a soul-energy *originating* on the soul plane. Feeling appreciation is one of the quickest ways to actually *connect* to the soul plane for the energetic benefit of yourself and others.

Write down...

what you like about life

what you like about sleeping

what you like about your five senses

what you might like about death

what you like about your friends and/or spouse

what you like about children

what you like about governments

what you like about landscapes and countrysides

what you like about yourself

what you like about your profession and/or expertise

what you like about one hundred other things

Note: This is not the exercise "write down what you like" (which is also a valid appreciation-technique in its own right) or "write down what you want", but an exercise in writing down what you like about other already existing things. Do intensify your level of appreciation throughout life and everything does indeed go more smoothly and prosperously. Put out love, get back love.

4. Color Levels

This is done as a meditation while lying down with your eyes closed.

Visualize yourself as a hollow/empty space and the universe as radiant white. Now fill this hollow space with the whole universe, pump yourself up with the white color. This will take 30 seconds to 2 minutes. Simply immerse yourself in that one color, have everything, including the inside of your body, your body, the room you are in and everything else be that color.

Next, let go of this impression and proceed to do the same thing with the color yellow.

Proceed with blue and then with violet.

The primary purpose of this is to activate forgotten soul memories. It might take awhile for such memories to trickle down to your conscious waking life self, but you have hereby triggered the process. Another result could be an awareness of the own evolutionary level (color) of your soul (if you do not experience a recognition of that, don't worry about it).

6

Mission of the Soul

In order to progress in life every soul reaches a point, sooner or later, where it will have to align it's desires as a soul with it's desires as an earth-being. Progress on a purely earthly mind-body level is limited. The beginner will view the physical universe as the most important thing. The medium-level soul will view the spiritual or non-physical universe as the most important thing. And the advanced soul will view both universes as important.

You can bring down a piece of the soul plane to earth my contemplation, learning, meditation, creativity and doing the things you most enjoy. By doing things you enjoy you are actually channelling soul plane energies to earth...by which you slightly open the amnesia filter.

If the soul has led a life it deems useful to itself and others it returns to the non-physical in an exuberant state. If it has wasted a life (by its own pre-defined standards) it returns wounded and usually admits to itself that it better have another incarnation in order to fulfil the goals originally set. Whether your Mission is completed can actually be felt. If you are feeling at all or in any way unsatisfied or compelled toward certain goals, your Mission on Earth is incomplete. If you feel completely at ease with all that is, your Mission is likely complete. Reincarnation is not a decision forced upon you but one you come to naturally. Souls grow up in an environment charged with such high vibration (love multiplied by thousands) that incarnation to earth always feels like a bit of a shock . Earth consciousness is about very raw, negative emotions such as anger, hate, fear, pain, survival and is an extreme contrast to the non-physical. Positive and negative energies are shared between soul and host (body). If the soul were only to know love and peace it would not learn contrast. The worse the life, the greater the *relief* afterwards. For souls who have led a peaceful life transit to the soul plane is more like a pleasant journey than full blown ecstasy One of the main original game goals however is to overcome negativity on the earth plane. The soul has repeated the game so many times that most souls will soon be ready to actually spend an entire life in joy (however tricky it may be to achieve that).

You have been taught by the mainstream but also by less than accurate spiritual teachings that your soul is *within* your body and that after death it is "outside" of the body, "leaves" the body. But actually there is a more accurate description that can be provided: The body exists *within* the soul. During life one *part* of the soul is identified with the body. The soul injects life, awareness, intelligence into the body but is not defined by the borders of the body. Another part of you is still and always discarnate and exploring realities outside of the body and the earth-plane. Nevertheless this identified part is under temporary amnesia concerning its other parts. The so-called "Out of Body Experience" is not actually that, but you merely becoming aware that you are already out of body and travel around there all the time.

After your talk with the Soul-Guide some Souls are indeed brought in front of some kind of panel, court or committee. This is described in biblical, ancient Tibetan and ancient Egyptian accounts. Witnesses have described this panel as superordinate, "wise elders", "archangels" and "directors" and consisting of three to ten members. No matter their verdict, it is always a reflection of your intentions and deeds during life. These are questioned and explored, but not condemned. Where do ideas such as "Judgment Day" and "Being Damned for Eternity" come from? They come from earthly consciousness misinterpreting these events, adding a fear-spin to what actually happens.

All souls, no matter their experience, finally arrive at some sort of "central gathering place" or "central hall" from which they continue Home. Sometimes souls are accompanied to this mass-transit space, sometimes the magnetic pull takes them here on their own. Just like we have airports, highways, train stations, cities, neighbourhoods, infrastructure, so does the soul-plane. It is here that the energy-field that the soul is, is "assigned" to their vibratory Home. Over many lifetimes the Home remains the same, unless there was a significant shift in vibration upwards or downwards, by which a new Home will be assigned. Usually the other Souls in your "Home Group" have similar goals to you and move upward with you. This is somewhat similar to school classes where some kids come and go, but a core group stays the same over the years. This transit-space is highly efficient and orderly and appears like thousands of highway crossings, but without traffic jams or accidents.

As already hinted at, you never incarnate with 100% of your energy. A part of you is really "left behind", but only both parts contain the entire information of your soul.. This is the reason you sometimes meet people on the soul plane that are still incarnate on some planet. And when you meet them, you also notice that they are not "fully here" in some odd way. Once your incarnation is done, you re-merge with the "left behind" part of you. This merging happens during your talk with the soul guide or upon arrival at home. The reason for some wanting to merge later is that the procedure of merging with the other part of yourself makes earth life seem more "unreal" and more difficult to recollect. They don't want to be talking to the Soul Guide without a clear recollection of what happened on Earth. Wanting to work on their last incarnation or meet other souls while still having fresh memories you wouldn't merge with your whole self too quickly. The more advanced a soul is, the less energy it takes with her/him into an incarnation and the more is left behind. Advanced Souls do have more energy in a sense, and only a droplet is enough to power an entire life.

From this luminous and awesome central crossroads premonitions of soon reuniting with very old friends arises. These very old friends that you will soon meet are your spiritual family and you had forgotten just how much you miss them. (On earth, your distant soul memory of this central hall is what makes you like airports). One thought is enough to establish telepathic affinity with those friends, before you even arrive Home. On soul-plane one thought is enough to establish telempathic affinity with your friends. Some are surprised when they can no longer get into telepathic contact with those they deemed family members. This is because not all of your earth family is also your soul family. You can only have this type of connection to your actual soul family. Your earthly family is a mixture of. Members of your real soul family but also beings who don't actually have anything to do with this core group. It has however happened that, because of your getting to know them on earth, they join your circle of friends.

Neither this central-space nor the soul-plane in general are the "darkness" normally associated with "infinite space". Everything constantly shines, shimmers, bounces, radiates. Central Hall is sometimes described as a place that moves when you move. Sensations of "floating" or "swimming" through it are not uncommon. These oceanic sensations are native to the entire soul-plane. The Happiness and inner Peace experienced have meanwhile reached an intensity ten times that of the initial afterlife moments.

Earth and other planets have imitated soul plane procedures, but the soul plane has imitated some physical-plane objects as well. Among souls there is a consensus that things like "Apples" never taste as good on the soul plane as on earth, where the idea originally comes from. Vice-versa, feeling love or even sexual intimacy never really reaches the intensity on earth that it does on the soul-plane. So there are many things "More Real" in the non-physical but still a few things "More real" in the physical. To claim that one of the realities is "an illusion" and the other not, is an obsolete notion. Yes, the non-physical is the source of the physical universe and thus superior to it but that doesn't make your life here "unreal". What is real or unreal is purely a matter of viewpoint. In any case you can create imitations of anything. Thought creates an immediate effect on this level. In physical space you need very, very, very, very much of that thought in order to create the reality of it or the equivalent physical action of that thought in order to give it "birth".

At your Home your soul group awaits you. As you approach your personal "cluster" identification and recognition is magnified manifold compared to your initial reception by relatives and friends. This moment is overwhelmingly divine and sweet, a taste of a Dimension even higher than the soul-plane you are currently on. As already mentioned, not all souls will be "fully present" because they are currently incarnate on some planet. These souls behave a bit like on "autopilot" or emanating a dimmer light and communicate a bit less then other souls.

After a brief welcome with *your* group you stand in front of the aforementioned committee (if you weren't already there) in order to explain your life. The talks with your soul guide where a preparation for your talks with the committee. Sometimes the soul guide accompanies you there acting as a kind of "lawyer" for your cause. I understand how some of this must sound like a far-out fantasy, but it reflects my own observations and those of thousands of others around the globe. Besides: Where do you think "Fantasy" comes from? The committee are almost always the same beings as those you had in previous discarnations, with only a minor exchange of employees over the millennia. The beings are described as souls themselves albeit taller, brighter and more majestic (as if it could get any more majestic!). Sometimes they communicate so quickly that you do not understand and require your soul guides translation. You will stand in front of them again before reincarnating.

Many people have the image of the soul plane being a place where you haphazardly or aimlessly fly around. If that's what you thought, think again. The place is beautifully structured and designed. Your home-group contains in average between three and thirty souls. This home group is part of a larger overall group (extended family) to which you have more lose relations. The overall group is again part of an even bigger cluster and so on. We will only look into your core-group here. Every member of your group has a different individuality, character and energy-field than you (although the general energy is similar enough to yours, otherwise you wouldn't belong to the same group). It seems to be more common that members of your group are spouses and sisters/brothers than your parents your children during incarnation. Quite a few souls seek out parents and/or children that do not directly relate to their own vibrational signal in order to gain new learning experiences. Another reason for this is that close friends are not that keen on showing up as an authority or caretaker during your incarnation.

The setting of a groups Home can take on an infinite number of variations. My own Soul-Group meets and studies in an environment that looks like a gigantic Greek temple. The extremely high and wide temple pillars have a blue glow. My own personal "soul level" is light-blue developing toward regular blue, and we feel the best at a home that displays many of the colors our energy body also has. Because my own level is light blue, my teachers will mostly be dark blue. My soul guide however, is dark violet...so dark violet that he/she is almost removed from this dimensional soul plane (on to higher business). Another aspect of my home is a vast deep blue ocean and something reminiscent of a beach scenery. Your cluster-home will have a different look and your soul family have other habits and appearances. Most souls of a group prefer to wear identities and certain genders over long periods of existence. In this sense you will meet "men and women". In my specific soul group we often meet at a library of the temple and flip through "books" which contain several of our lives. We might study various scenes or discuss future lives and possibilities. The "pictures" in these books are moving, three-dimensional action-pictures (movies in fact) that change throughout a scene. These types of "books" are common and widely reported among those channelling soul-plane memories. My group places value on plenty of humorous exchange by making fun of various inadequacies displayed during an incarnation. The entire group is usually fascinated at viewing the earth-life of a returnee because these lives make for divine comedy. The limitations and frustrations of earth are a cause of great laughter.

Some have asked whether you can leave your Group or Home. The answer is: It is possible to leave it for awhile or entertain contact to other groups but it doesn't happen too often because you feel "at home" with "your own people". This is a closer bond than most earthly families have because it contains common interests and intentions. Each core-group has a soul guide, sometimes two or three even. Every soul guide is assigned to more than one soul. Activities of a group do vary from person to person. Some spend time playing games that would seem strange from an earthly perspective. Some study past lives. Some plan optional future lives. Some continue their studies on the nature of existence. Some create objects that will later appear on some planet in the physical universe. Just like an earth mind may create a computer application for use in virtual reality, a soul may create a physical object for use in the physical universe.

Differences in color seem to indicate the souls level of consciousness or level of development, according to some accounts. Infinity is designed in a way that there is actually no limit to expansion and growth and once you've reached the "highest" and "most illuminated" state, there's always something more to be discovered. The souls development stage and color is mostly connected to the number of incarnations it has had, but it doesn't have to be. There are souls you have had numerous incarnations but still haven't made any "progress" and shine innocent white, and then there's souls who glow purple after only a few. So where to those innocent and lovely new souls originate from, you ask? That' s a secret I will not disclose here. Find it out for yourself when on the soul plane.

Level 1: **Beginner soul**. White, bright, homogeneous Status as soul guide: None.

Level 2: **Lower Mid-Level**. White mixed with other colors (yellow, orange, red). Status as soul guide: Zero.

Level 3: **Mid-Level:** Solid yellow without a mix of other colors, without any white). Status as soul-guide: Zero.

Level 4: **Upper Mid-Level:** Dark Yellow or deep Gold (sometimes a green shimmer or tendencies toward blue). Status as soul guide: In Junior Training.

Level 5: **Advanced Level.** Light blue (without yellow, sometimes tending to deeper blue). Status as soul guide: Yes, can be and sometimes is a soul guide.

Level 6: **Very Advanced Level.** Dark Blue. Status as soul guide: Expert.

Level 7: **Extremely Advanced:** Color: Violet. Status as soul guide: Master.

Level 8: **Beyond Advanced:** Color: Dark Violet or Purple (surrounded by radiant light): Status as soul guide: Beyond.

On this particular soul plane there are no further higher or lower levels, these seem to be the ones defined. A "lower" level might be "the birth of individuality" (which we will not go into here not only because I want you to find out for yourself but also because I myself do not quite understand the process of soul birth as a ball of energy. There are indeed many, many things I don't understand. And I distrust any spiritual teacher who claims to have it "all figured out"). A higher level than dark violet would include the shift to another dimensional domain, which is beyond the scope of this chapter.

If for some reason we had to classify the levels without colors we could do so by behavior, conduct, statements and interests as well or by our "sense" of someone. These classifications into color and rank can be misleading from a world-mind perspective. The evolutionary steps of a soul do not actually describe "worse" and "better", "higher and lower" or even progression over linear time but rather the "experience-density" of the soul. But how is one to explain that to the earth-mind who sees everything in linear terms?

The white beginner-souls have the same options and abilities as the advanced ones. They too are able to jump dimensions, they too can create, they too can practice free will, they too can participate in a myriad of games and universes. The classifications serve to show who has organizational authority on a certain level and this is determined by experience. Compared to all-that-is, even this soul plane is small (even if its much bigger than the physical universe) and *in relation to infinity all souls are almost "on the same level".* Discernments could be expanded or compressed as needed. Being a "yellow" soul puts you much closer to a "violet" soul than that violet soul is to beings from other circles of infinity.

If you wish to know what color-stage your soul is on, ask yourself which color you felt the most attracted to before reading all of this. It wasn't a surprise to me when, awhile ago, someone told me my soul is light blue. Before that I had always been attracted by blue, liking to wear blue. People dressed "dark blue" I viewed as "authorities" when I was a child - soul memories trickling through the amnesia. My light-blue status also shows why I am able to support and strengthen some people (souls that are either also light-blue or below) and others not (violet and white are outside of my common vibratory reach). We rarely get into personal contact with souls that are outside of our range anyway. Funny thing is that there are souls on significantly higher frequencies than me who have become so immersed in amnesia that they don't realize it. These are people that eventually support/strengthen me though, although initially it may not look like it. People attracted to this type of reading material are usually the blue and gold types.

The levels of energy presented in my book of the same name don't necessarily have a relation to the souls color because advanced souls may or may not choose to reside in high levels of consciousness on earth. The soul-plane relates to the levels in that the lower astral goes from 0 to 199, the mid- and higher-astral from 200 to 499 and the celestial from 500 to 1000. Beyond the 1000 a higher Dimension begins. This is the linear way of viewing the Universe.

A brief note on the subject of "evil". The influence of "evil" and things such as "hell" and ill-mannered "demons", "punishment after life", "desperation" and "realities there is no escape from" are overblown and overestimated on the earth plane. We've invested more attention into it than it deserves. These ideas do not originate from higher planes. The higher soul plane is not a duality of dark and light, good and evil but 100% pure positive energy. It is only the more dense physical plane that creates negativity and projects some of these ideas to higher planes. This is how a committee becomes a tribunal, an anomaly of energy becomes "demon possession" and a low vibratory plane becomes "hell". Evil is indeed a creation of this vibratory universe of extreme duality and not a characteristic of the soul plane. Yes, it is possible to create and experience extreme levels of insanity, but only by getting into vibratory correspondence with such realities. Thus, the lower-astral region was originally created by thought-forms on earth and not by the soul-plane. Souls who develop such leanings are a rarity and are handled on the soul plane in the following manner: They are isolated from their group for a certain period of time so that they can live out and act out their horror visions (which they attracted themselves to by means of exaggerated *fascination* with the subjects...whether this fascination was projected wittingly or unwittingly), and are occasionally offered healing. In very, very, very, very rare and exceptional cases there is an overlapping of dimensions in which certain stray beings from other universes or parallel worlds accidentally show up in our universe. Some of these beings are so strange and different from our own universe that they appear as "very evil" to our tastes and understanding. As infinity is a big place there are of course other beings and frameworks...some of which we'd rather not meet. But these being so foreign to the human experience, you needn't meet or see any of it...ever. You only attract that which you are interested in. And even attracting actual evil entities from foreign universes requires more than mere attention (what it requires need not be shared, for obvious reasons). The recommendation for anyone is not to take evil seriously, not to take it as important as it can only survive within your field of perception by giving it meaning/importance/reality. Planet earth has a class of people that use "evil" as a tool for inducing fear so that they can manipulate them. This is the main source of "evil". Religious leaders would have some difficulty gathering followers if they wouldn't be continuously focusing on and creating "evil". The formula applied is PRS – Problem Reaction Solution. In applying this formula you present a problem to people, they react emotionally to it and then you offer the solution. Problem and Solution are created by the same source (either unwittingly or by masking it). The solution is mostly something one wants to sell or force down peoples throats but couldn't if the artificial "problem" weren't created first. Some examples.

The strange thing is that Problem and Solution are often created by the same source. What's even stranger is that some people/groups know what they are doing and do it deliberately. Normally you'd be creating the problem subconsciously in order to sell the solution (like I imply that the world needs my books in order to sell them) but some black sheep of our global family know exactly what they are doing and artificially exaggerate the problem in order to have more people calling for their "solution". The technique is very ancient and it's still being "successfully" used to this day.

The only protection from low vibes and lower astral realms is love. If you are a kind and loving being you will not even get in range of evil peripherally.

The Mission of your Soul is interlinked to the Mission of your Soul-Guide. There are no known cases in which a soul does not have a Guide. Guides are assigned to that human by a mysterious superordinate source. Some of them are closer to the incarnate humans than others. Some Guides believe in leaving a soul to his own, while others try to positively intervene at various points in life. It really depends on what you and your soul guide have planned for your life and what their Philosophy is. On an earth-plane if you feel a certain "presence" near you or something "protective" ("guardian angel"), this is the Soul-Guide. It is more easily perceivable in states of

Meditation and Deep Calm or states of Emergency than in regular daily life. Any time you are deeply relaxed and in deep trouble, the channels to your soul guide are wide open (In emergency cases the soul guide is equipped to perform "miracles" if you call out for them).

Re-cognizing the soul guide is not too difficult since you are connected since millenia. Re-connecting with them, adds an additional Dimension of warmth, creativity and safety to your earthly life. It is not planned to have frequent contact. But since you are reading this information it means that you were meant to read it, you were lead to it. And maybe your Soul Guide led you to it, so that you get back in touch for an update or two. The meaning of your life becomes more apparent through this connection.

The Soul Guides advanced Consciousness makes him an intricately mysterious, fascinating and very able being who is equipped with w wide range of techniques, methods, tricks and viewpoints to train and support you. This is your own personal "Yoda", so to speak.

Soul guides are *not* your "Higher Self", but often mistaken with that. Higher Self is simply yourself, your soul without all the earthly baggage, without the amnesia, without a brain and body. You will make a jump in understanding when you understand that your soul is not "within" your body, but your body is *within* your soul, ore more precisely: Your body is an *extension* of your soul, a densification of it. It can be very limiting to think that your soul is located inside your head or body. These are earthly limitations that are just plain wrong. Because the soul plane *encompasses* the physical plane, the earth plane is only its outermost peak. I repeat this because this basic understanding automatically leads to other intuitions and realizations throughout time. Soul Guides more often communicate with and address Higher Self than world-self. So oftentimes it is as if the Messages from your Guide are Received through your Higher Self or what you call Intuition. As far as the world-self is concerned, Soul Guide and Higher Self are therefore nearly identical. Whether your Guidance is coming from Guide or Higher Self is then secondary.

Intuition does not explain. Intuition does not follow logic. Intuition does not always look reasonable. Intuition only points the way. Its whisper is soft. It says "that direction" or "this direction". Sometimes it is drowned out by the noise of daily life and the world-mind. In calm intuition can be heard just fine. Intuition sometimes makes suggestions that others wouldn't understand if you explain it to them.

Today I did not change the lanes on the Highway although someone was flashing his headlights for me to get out of the way so that he could pass. Normally I always make way. But not this time. I was asked: "Why don't you get out of the way? Someone wants to pass you!". This question was answered the very moment a car suddenly shifted from the 1st lane to the second...where I would have been had I switched. The accident would have been deadly. Looking that the car I responded: "That's why".

This happens all the time when you're in a calm state. You "just know". "Just Because".

Soul-Guides are not your Soulmates or Soulfriends. Although your soul mates are, to some extent, able to support you from the soul plane, they rarely do. Most of your soul friends are on the same development level as you. In rare cases the soul guide incarnates at the same time you do and may appear as a "friend" or "wise mentor" but he is still different than a soul mate.

Advanced souls have the energy to lead many lives at once. They incarnate into and occupy more than one body – at the same time. These bodies may be located in different dimensions, lives, times, planets. This is different than there existing many versions of yourself as described in my book "Parallel Universes of Self". The concept here refers to a soul being in many different people, and the parallel-universes book refers to different *versions* of one person. To combine the Parallel Universes concept with the concept of densities from soul-plane down to the Physical Universe. The densities can be seen as many concentric circles, and the parallel-universes as many such circle-objects stacked up beside or on-top of each other. This may be somewhat difficult for an earth-mind to grasp.

Another fascinating ability of Advanced Souls is that they are able to incarnate without first being born. The earthly term for this is "walk-in". While rather uncommon on earth (and I wouldn't give that much credence to people who claim they are walk-ins), it is common practice on other planets.

Some of the thoughts you consider your own are actually from Higher Self or Soul Guide. 99% of your thinking is created by your earth-self, but a small part is filtered down from on up. You recognize such Communications in dreams when something is said to you *by another being* that touches you or seems oddly relevant to a broader perspective. Some Communication is delivered through "funny/strange coincidences". The soul guide and the higher self appear "playful" and "humorous" compared to the world-self. Being humorous and light yourself rather than stuck and serious, they have an easier time getting through to you as well.

One of the ways my Higher Self plays with me is through name-synchronicity. Names always come in pairs in my email box. So for a while I will be dealing with a bunch of Davids. Then, later, I will be corresponding with a bunch of Larrys. And then with a bunch of Janets. And so on. I've shown this pattern in my emails to some people and they couldn't believe their eyes. This has been going on since years. When one person of a certain name writes to me, other people of that name also start writing. What does it mean? Nothing – except that Higher Self has a sense of Humor and is making their presence known.

A few of the more cheeky soul guides use shock or accidents to wake you up to certain things. For people who are very religious, soul guides have to *pose* as religious figures in to make contact. We are only indirectly accountable to all-that-is or the Supreme Being none as God. We are more directly accountable to ourselves and the Soul Guide after the body dies. In other words, what we call God, is less personal than the earth-mind makes it out to be. These mentors called Soul-Guides are more personal. One could say they are Gods representatives. I guess this paragraph also settles whether I believe in God or not: Yes, I absolutely believe in a Grand, Glorious and Supreme Creator. In my experience God is both all that is and the source of all that is. This is no contradiction from a higher perspective. There are many levels of superordinate energies, but God is the Ultimate Source, the Infinite and Eternal, the only thing that is constant. (A hint: If you want to know what is "more real" as opposed to "less real", look at what is most unchanging).

Soul-Guides are mostly assigned to us because they have mastered an art with which we are stuck. Sometimes it needs a few thousand years to incorporate certain lessons but these "long time spans" are not that long in terms of the superordinate domain. Not all advanced souls become Soul-Guides. Some take on other tasks. And not all souls incarnate, much less on planet earth. The descriptions provided in this chapter mostly refer to the lives and afterlives of earth-beings, of human-centered experiences, which is one of many games within Infinity.

The Soul-Guide is pure loyalty. Earthly concepts of "giving up", "leave someone", "deny support" and "not liking someone" do not exist for it. This does not mean that the Soul Guide is a yea-sayer and follows every command of yours. They are enigmatic, mysterious beings and decide for themselves which pieces of information they give you and which they withhold. You will experience them as very cooperative at times and at other times they will simply observe without intervening at all. Some are tight lipped with information. This also has to do with your *true or hidden intentions* and what you radiate. If you have the feeling that the "powers that be" (your soul guide) are not acting in your best interest, then examine your own intentions and check *if* they are in your best interest, because the soul guide is only loyal to your true intentions (from a soul-perspective) and not your temporary ego-moods (from an earthly-perspective).

They never move far away enough for them to become strangers to us, but sometimes they will tend to make themselves scarce if we are in a life phase of denial (unwilling to confront problems and their solutions). They do not want to and will not support us until we've given the initiating impulse for certain changes. So contrary to popular opinion, they do not "always come when you call". They perceive every call, but do not answer to any. This is found in the wisdom of "Help yourself first, then God will help you". The only source of help that is always present is your own soul, which does actually have the power to handle every situation. You will actually never experience anything that is beyond what you can bear. That would contradict the "law of correspondence/attraction". You are constantly emitting thought-pulses. If your Guide were to react to each of them, it would not be a good mentor. Its "protective hand" is only necessary for less advanced souls. A completely stable soul will not "call the gods" at every little ache and pain but apply its own God-given abilities. If you are the boss of a company and have given your employee everything he needs to do his work, you will not respond to his calls of "needing a pen" because you have given the employee not only half a dozen pens but also knowledge of where to get new pains if the old ones run out.

In times of intense suffering, intense indecisiveness, melancholy of the heart or in times of great zeal, great focus and great joy and times of great change, you can be sure that the soul guide is a bit more attentive and a bit closer. Furthermore, you can contact your "higher coach" in meditation or deep relaxation, when the censoring mind is half-asleep. The question to ask yourself before contacting your soul guide is if you really need him/her, if it is really that important and if there is really something you could do if you had an answer to something. There is no sense in tapping higher non-physical energy and information, if you do not use the answers given on a physical plane. So before contacting higher sources: *What do you intend to do with the information/energy given? If you do not use it for your physical life, why should the information be given to you?*

I have watched those who have climbed certain spiritual heights, opened certain channels of higher level communication...and then don't do anything with it. Then they are surprised that the "channels to heaven" eventually run dry. If they are not used for arts (music, acting, painting, dancing) nor for teaching nor for managing a company nor for anything else there is no point in achieving them. So indeed, you will experience higher states and more communication with higher intelligences if you actually *do* something with it, if you actually bring it down to earth. But if you are currently surfing the Internet or in the living room having smalltalk with your relatives over a cup of coffee... *what do you need a state of enlightenment for?* You don't. That's why you will only receive energy and information when you need it. A few years ago I asked my Soul Guide (on the soul plane) why I don't experience the states of bliss I used to experience in my early twenties. He showed me what I was doing in those magical states: Walking around shopping malls, sitting around with friends, sitting in front of the computer. And he asked me "Do you need these states for such activities?`" He then reminded me of the fact that I still experience these states now and then. The last time I skyrocketed up the scale of consciousness was when I stood in front of a group of 200 people holding a speech on Spirituality. It was there just when I needed it. Having a state just for states sake will not do. The energy has to *flow* somewhere. So be happy and satisfied if you are in "medium" states of energy while doing "medium" things in your day. Regular support does not come from the Guide anyway. It only provides advanced instruction. Your regular support and navigation systems are your emotions, feelings, intuitions...which are communications from your own Soul, translated by the body.

Techniques and Meditations

1. **Personal Paradise**

Note: This technique first appeared in Level 2 of the Reality Creation Course at oceanofsilence.com

"Personal Paradise" is a technique that allows you to contact higher-self and your soul guide without the help of hypnotherapy, channelling or out-of-body-travel.

Where is paradise?

Paradise is within you. As long as your circumstances and immediate surroundings do not show a paradise full of prosperity, peace and happiness, you have to go get it yourself by finding it within. If you want to improve your life this is a priority, because only giving your attention to what is already manifest in your surroundings, only creates more of what already IS. "Paradise is within" is not just a metaphor, but is meant literally.

In many schools of therapy and spirituality it is popular to conduct so called "guided imagery" and "trance journeys". We intend to do something similar here, but with a few subtle differences, with a different understanding and different intentions. Normally inner journeys are undertaken to "relax" or "access the subconscious". These exercises are often done in the presupposition that Imagination is only that….Imagination, compared to the "real world" you "return" to when you open your eyes. Or that "relaxing" is only relaxing…quite pleasant but without real consequences in physical reality. We say that relaxing and imagining is much more than that.

We don't label imagination as something unreal, non-solid, non-consistent, vague (it only becomes intangible if you don't give it any attention), but as the very source of physical reality. Anything you can imagine does exist on some level and on that level it is just as real and valid as your physical surroundings and your body. Within this practice it is a required to soften your judgement on what imagination "means". Labelling Imagination as "unreal" will devitalize and disable your Imaginations influence on reality. So while you dwell in your personal paradise, do not even label it as "imagination", but simply enjoy it just as you would enjoy any other paradise. Its an *Experience* and consciousness will conceive it as such.

When we go on a journey of imagination then, we do that:

1. not in order to "make something happen later", but to experience something as real **Now**.
2. not in order to "get access to the subconscious" but to get access to our Higher Self and the entire universe.
3. not only to relax, but to give up our entire impatience and resistance toward anything. To relax deeply and regenerate fully.
4. not only to open up to potential or to change perception or attitude, but to change entire reality.

This practice is based on the notion that "its all happening within". Whatever is happening within is what is happening in your entire universe and your immediate physical surroundings are only a tiny part of all-that-is-happening within your universe.

Later on, in your meditation, take an imaginary trip to your "Personal Paradise". Your personal paradise that you create within the world of your mental imagery and emotions is a place to which you want to keep returning and includes recognizable traits, symbols, objects, sounds, temperatures, feelings. An archetype of this Meditation would, for instance, be a beach at the ocean. Beaches are associated with freedom and relaxation. Of course you can choose another place that represents truth, beauty, freedom, regeneration for you.

This will be a place you visit repeatedly, a place you retreat to regenerate, refresh, centre yourself, re-charge. The more often you visit the place, the more a mere symbolic place of relaxation and freedom becomes an energetic reality of relaxation and freedom. By continuing to return to the place you "charge" the thought so that later on a few minutes of visitation there will be enough for many days of having energy or being in the flow.

Once your personal paradise is sufficiently "charged" and filled with meaning and importance, visiting it *replaces* many other efforts to improve your state. It becomes a ritual, a regular part of your life. And over time you can add anything to it that you associate with high energy, high vibration or your ideal self.

A part of your personal paradise is the "Round Table". That's where you go and sit down when you want to communicate with your ideal self, your higher self or your inner coach / mentor. Meetings at the Round Table are not done on every trip to your personal paradise but only on some. Its where you go when you want to solve problems, ask questions, achieve things and discuss them with higher sources of wisdom. This method represents the utilization of the highest versions of yourself. Communication with these energies begins as imagination but condenses to more and more concrete realities over time so that guidance from above and pleasant surprises and pointers will also start showing up in your dreams and everyday life.

Visit your personal paradise on a regular basis, the personal paradise that can only be found within *you*, to stay there for a while or to retreat there when life is no more fun. This has nothing to do with "escaping reality" but with shifting it. If your everyday life is no more fun, you needn't continue to give it attention by fighting against it. Instead, embrace your daily life as best you can, and also provide attention to something more pleasant, and eventually, more pleasant things will happen in your everyday life. This is the art and secret of creating a new reality.

The added value to this practice is that you also meet with higher aspects of Consciousness. These can be symbolized as higher self, beings from another world, a coach or anything else you can talk to. In advanced versions of this, you can even identify and merge with an ideal self after finishing your talk with him/her. You can take his/her/its place, BE it, feel it, see from its eyes. The more familiar you become with being another version of yourself, the more this spills over into real life.

The "Personal Paradise" Meditation summarizes many different benefits into one single practice:

1. Training your attention/concentration
2. Training your Imagination
3. Connecting to your Higher Self

4. Relaxation and Regeneration
5. Creating a higher vibration (through which you attract other things in your life)

If it is not going well in your everyday life, you'll do good to retreat to your paradise. Any type of boredom, frustration, confusion or anger is a good reason to stop looking for a solution "out there" and instead look into yourself. Amazing answers are waiting for you at the round table of your paradise. Sometimes you will notice how the answers are created by you, and sometimes they really do come from a Higher Source. But even if you notice how you the answers are coming from you, they are much better answers because you are in a higher state of awareness during your meditation. Your inner coach will deliver much better answers than an outside coach could ever. Better answers than Wikipedia and Google. Better answers than parents, teachers, friends. It might be advisable to make notes after your session, as the answers received in a higher state of being are sometimes forgotten after returning back from your semi-trance.

Change the landscape of your personal paradise slowly and over the course of time. Changing it too quickly will not allow it to "charge up" and gain referential meaning and hold in your mind. When you do change it you can invite new friends there, create new methods of refreshment (a fountain of youth for example), build something there, get rid of weed (symbolizing getting rid of problems), etc. All this starts working once you give up the label "its only imagination". Repeated visits will make it stronger and stronger and stronger, its effect on your thinking, feeling and acting will become more and more obvious and the events you magnetically attract more and more joyful.

2. Contacting Higher-Self and/or Soul Guide through Intention

For those seeking "an easier way" to establish contact: Simply define the subject you would like support for. This might be a decision you want guidance for or it might be something you want to know about your life's purpose. Then define what you are going to do with the information given to you. If that is defined then it wont be a big problem getting some guidance. Your

Communication is done in written form, verbally or mentally. It can be phrased in many different ways:

* "I call upon the Most High..."

* "Dear God, I ask..."

* "Hello there, Higher Self, I would like to make a request..."

* "Soul-Guide, if you indeed do exist, I would appreciate..."

My own tone with these energies is mostly conversational.

After "filing your request" speak or write the words: "*Thank you for showing me that this issue is already resolved*". The answer you are seeking will come in the form of a "coincidence", an "omen", a dream at night, a prickling or tickling sensation somewhere in the body or feeling a presence near you. Sometimes the answer comes through an unexpected unfolding of events. While these events may not obviously connect to your request at first, it does eventually become very obvious and unambiguous that there is a connection.

3. Deactivating Problem-Reaction-Solution traps

The purpose of this exercise is to protect you from manipulation.

a) Write down the names of people and organizations that have offered you help and solutions when you really needed them (on a separate piece of paper)

b) Afterwards, look at your list and differentiate between situations where you made an informed decision about wanting something and situations where people were telling you had a problem that they could solve.

c) Then, define from which of these sources you no longer need help because you either feel confident that you can solve it yourself or because it is no longer a problem.

Finally, contemplate these questions for a few minutes:

What are some problems in this world, and who is *benefiting* from them?

Who would become unemployed if certain problems didn't exist anymore?

4. Contacting the Soul

Another way to contact higher sources of energy and information is by reading this section while you apply the exercises described. In order to read this section you will therefore need two hours of time and a silent, undisturbed space where you can lie down and keep putting this writing aside to implement the techniques.

Lie down or sit for this meditation, these writings loosely in your hand. If you tend to fall asleep during exercises, then sit. If you tend to tense up, then lie. Let this book lie somewhere beside your body for the duration of the three hours. *You will be taking the paper into your hand for one paragraph, then putting it aside to do the exercise, then taking it again for the next paragraph, and so on.*

In the first 15 minutes, establish neutral attention. That means you are lying there and breathing, but you quit anything other than observing. Breathing softly and deeply and slowly, observing, without desire, preference, avoidance, resistance, reaction, anything. Allow peace and silence to pervade. Notice the silence of the space you are in. Silence of the mind. A peaceful ocean. Let thoughts "run their course" and eventually phase-out, by doing nothing with them anymore. Let events of the day run their course and phase-out. In the first 15 minutes of your meditation, give everything up that you "know" or "expect". (As you are at the end of your paragraph, this is the point where you put this paper aside and follow suit for 15 minutes before picking it up again).

Allow inner happiness, an inner smile, inner well-being to flow in. For this you may use imagery or imagination, or simply your intention to allow. Label the happiness you feel as "level 1 happiness" and allow yourself to let in this feeling tenfold (level 10 happiness). Then allow it to go to level 100 happiness. Then level 1000. And if you are thinking "this is currently the outermost limit of joy I am able and willing to let in, then allow even more anyway. Go to level 10 000. The numbers are only an analogous anchor and don't have to be followed with precision. The point of this is to gently and slowly allow more and more ecstasy to flow through your body, mind and being. And when you have reached the high-point, to expand your limits even more. 10 000 is the uttermost you can do? Then allow 100 000. And 1 Million. And 10 Million. And 1 Billion. And 1 Trillion particles of joy...in which ever way is good for you. And when you think "Wow...this is the happiest I have *ever* been", then become even happier still. And when you have, by far, exceeded the outer and uppermost happiness...let go, let your mind become empty and just relax back into neutral attention, no matter what feeling-reverberations or lingering emotions are still there. This is done for about 10 minutes.

Perceive yourself as a body and an energy-form that is bigger than your body. Perceive your energy form as the double length and the double width of your body. You do this with the help of your imagination. Be luminous and radiant white energy, pulsate white, fill yourself with white, merge with white, let white flow through you, feel pure, fresh and white light. Do this for about 5 minutes.

Relax and consider that you are, energetically speaking, now an entirely different person in an entirely different world than 30 minutes ago. The person lying or sitting here is not the same person you were. This person has changed his/her energy and therefore *is* another person. Even if the physical universe around you seems to be the same, it is not, because you are another person. Things "staying the same" is an illusion of the mind. Actually, even if you would not have done this meditation up to now, you would be a completely different person than 30 minutes ago, because the sense of time-continuity is also an illusion, similar to the illusion of separate film-strips being "one" film strip in "continuity". You believe in this illusion because the film-strips go by faster than your eye can view them as separate. "Daily life" happens in a very similar way (except that it is three-dimensional whereas the film-strips are two-dimensional and the soul-plane is four-dimensional). You are a completely different person than before. Now, take in a fixed viewpoint outside of or above your body and observe your body "from above", observe it lying there. Remain in this viewpoint, be this viewpoint in the air and observe things from there. 5 minutes.

Now that you are back to reading, your viewpoint is back inside your head. Next you will return to and stay in the viewpoint in the air, above your body and stabilize that viewpoint by deciding that you are not your body but the purely mental viewpoint, pure consciousness, pure awareness. Float in the air for half a minute or a minute, and then *turn around*, no longer facing your body lying there, but other things, the room in which you are, maybe looking out of the window. Remain in this viewpoint outside of your body and look around (the eyes of your body are closed). From this viewpoint perceive an object in your surroundings (which you don't take as "imagination" but as perception). Examine the object. Say "hello" to the object. Let the object softly say "hello" back to you. Get closer to the object with the intention to explore it. Go inside the object, merge with it, become it, identify with it. Feel it, feel what it feels like, explore it from inside. Now *be* the object and observe the world from the eyes of the object. If it makes it easier for you, whisper "I am _____ (insert object name)". Observe the body lying over there (your former body) from the eyes of your new body (the object). Remain in this new viewpoint, looking around, for about 5 minutes (This entire section taking about 7 Minutes).

You have just taken this piece of writing back into your hands, but try to remain somewhat identified with the object. Next you will leave the object, leave the room in which the object and your former body are lying. The room and the building it is in become smaller and smaller and smaller and smaller as you fly into space and take in a viewpoint in space (no matter how you imagine this). 1 Minute.

Expand the size of your own being to encompass and contain everything that exists. First you are a point within space and then space is within you. This is as if you are a balloon that is blown up so much that it contains the entire universe and everything inside it. Give yourself up to 3 minuets for this.

Everything is now within you, so ask yourself what is *behind* you. Turn around very quickly, very suddenly. Remain in neutral-attention mode and simply wait what happens, what comes up for up to 30 seconds.

Create a symbolic or imagined representation of your soul guide. Let this representation be precious, wonderful, noble, magical in appearance. You are creating a shape or form through which your actual soul guide can appear and communicate. Then wait in silence while expecting your soul guide to merge with this form/shape, being grateful that you have provided the appropriate space in which he/she can "come through". 1 Minute.

Have a conversation with your soul guide. This communication can be in imagery, verbally, emotionally or symbolically. Do this up to 10 minutes.

End the conversation or Q&A session by thanking your soul guide. Return slowly to the planet earth, the building you were in, the room, and back into your physical body. Lie there and remain relaxed. 1 Minute.

Speak out loud: "I now remember the most important points of my past lives". Keep your eyes closed and just lie there and wait for images and imagination-flashes to come up *spontaneously and by themselves*. Do not intentionally imagine something. You might repeat the statement one, two or three times. 3 Minutes.

Speak out loud: "I do not remember the most important points of my past lives". Repeat this three times. Linger and check what doubts and counter-thoughts arise to the statement that you cannot remember. 3 Minutes.

Speak out loud: "I now remember the residence of my soul between lives. I do remember my last discarnation." Linger and lie and just wait for what spontaneous images come up. 3 Minutes.

Speak out loud: "I now remember my plans and my soul mates for this life". And linger, breathe and wait for what comes up. 3 Minutes.

Open your eyes and write. Write down what you remember or feel or intuit. Even write down mere vague thought-flashes without any evaluation of whether they are "real" or "important". If anything strange happened or if new thoughts came up. Every single thought you had during the last 15 minutes counts. 3 Minutes.

While it is difficult getting information "they" (we) want to keep secret from us, we can still do this by beginning with "little pieces". Maybe you even received more than little pieces during this session. By focussing on the little pieces, they accumulate and more and more reveals itself. Sometimes the information you receive because of the preceding meditation does not arrive immediately...but over weeks...unexpectedly, while you are not looking. Put everything that you *assume* about your past lives, lives as a soul, intentions as a soul, communications from your soul guide, every little possible hint and thought-snippet on your written list. While writing this list you will attract more thoughts and extrapolations – because the writing has focused your attention – add these new thoughts to your list.

Once your list is finished, choose items from the list that interest you (interest is an indicator that you can found out more about something), and think about that item for a bit, consider it, check what you *associate* with it. What new thoughts come up when looking at those thoughts? Write down these too, add them to your list. If something is not relevant or true or will most likely not yield any results, you will not be interested in it or it will not produce emotions. Most of the things that did come up during this entire meditation are somewhat relevant for you however...*otherwise they wouldn't have come up.* That's why for the duration of this exercise, you leave aside all scepticism Just because some memory "doesn't make sense" to you does not mean that it has nothing to do with you. The very fact that it "doesn't make sense" to you shows that it is a memory from beyond your filter of amnesia. Consider it and its meaning will become more clear. The collection of puzzle-pieces you have gathered here are a good beginning that will facilitate changes within your energy-body that happen by themselves. In other words, it is not necessary to keep pounding upon "getting more" information. Whatever *was* delivered is good enough for now, giving you just what you need. Collecting data from beyond the amnesia threshold can be done in many different ways. If you have your own ways and means to do that, by all means go ahead.

7

Choosing Your Incarnation

Every soul chooses its next Life. This occurs in collaboration with the Soul-Guide and a space in which "possible future lives" can be viewed as if in a cinematic experience. Thousands of people recall residing in such a space that resembles a huge, multi-dimensional movie and sound-studio, complete with mixer and editing devices. I know how strange this might sound, but that is pretty much the consensus among experiencers. This space is operated by some other person who collaborates with you and the Soul-Guide. A screen is shown in which different variations of lives are played. You watch different life options, rewind them, freeze-frame them, forwards wind them and even check different possible branch-offs of any given life. You can also test what impact different choices would have on the movie. This room or space is one of the most stunning I have experienced anywhere. The "movies" have a strange realistic fluidity to them and while there you can witness the movie-like nature of reality first hand. The choice of movies are only limited to which lessons you as a soul want to run through and the recommendations of your Soul-Guide. So instead of being able to choose between millions of lives, your choice is reduced to about a dozen. But these dozen lives are not fixed and within each of them, there are endless variations, parallel possibilities and branch-offs which can be experienced. If it has been determined that a person dies at the age of 23, then the energies are aligned according to that. But...the decisions you make here or during your incarnation can still be circumvented or retracted. The mix of pre-determined ("destiny") and free-will options is what makes life unpredictably fascinating. It's even possible to choose an entirely new life purpose *during* your incarnation if the "lessons to be learned" have been completed earlier than planned. Normally someone only dies after he has had the experience he came here for. Example: If someone was a bloodthirsty and arrogant tyrant in his last life, then it is recommended that he balance that out with the opposite in his next life and he will incarnate as a meek servant. If however, this lesson was accepted without resistance so that already at the age of 20 you have fully experienced the "meek servant" identity, then your lesson is learned and you could die. Or you define a *new lesson* and enjoy the rest of your stay on the planet.

In this space, you can choose who your parents will be, what you will look like, which profession you will probably have, what gender you will have, where you are born and into which type of vibratory environment you are born. This space is not about pre-determination but all about probability. And so you explore various lives of people you might be on the screen. In this sense (and this is really awesome) the screen is a time-machine in which you travel forward and backward in time. The movie and screen are not flat like we know them but have a strange fluid and multi-dimensional quality to them. When you re-wind or wind-forward it is as if you are rewinding water-waves or "fluid pictures". I recall being able to operate the "mixer" myself. I also recall my Soul-Guide censoring what I saw on screen once, because knowing that would have interfered with my stated Intentions for that life.

An example: You tell your Soul-Guide that you want to be a musician in your next life, in Canada. And you want to be a man. So then it is the room operators job to find options that come close to what you would like. But even here, choices are limited. Also, you have agreed to limit your money for the beginning in order to heighten creativity. So it has been arranged that you will only have money after the mid-point of your life. The options are limited because there are a limited amount of babies being born with these traits. Finally someone is found in Montreal, albeit a family that only speaks Canadian-French, although you preferred to incarnate speaking English In an English-language region of town there is also an English-speaking family but they are too rich for your intended purposes. So you watch the movie of that person which shows you some significant moments of the persons life and some smaller moments. You get an overall impression of what it is like to be that person. None of the events are "fixed" in anyway. The only thing that is fixed is the overall and general identity and starter-environment. If you say "Alright...this is similar to the person I want to be", then that incarnation will be arranged. If you say "No, I want something else", the room operator has to keep searching. The most fantastic feature of these "movies" is that you can either watch them from outside (dissociated) or step into certain scenes yourself in order to "try them on". Have you ever had the desire to "step into a movie"? Well...you have done this *many times* on the soul plane.

The *desires* you have in life are limited to the identity you have chosen. If you have chosen the identity "musician" you will not feel the real desire to become a president (And if you do then its not really a desire but an illusion implanted into you by society). That desire can be fulfilled if you be-lieve in it (rather than only desiring it). It's as simple as that. You cannot hold the feeling of having something and not experience it. With one exception: If there is a deeper layer of belief that *you do not wish to disturb*, your desire will not come true, or more precisely, you will not fully identify with or allow yourself to feel a certain reality. That deeper layer of belief is saying that "If I create Y, then I have to sacrifice X and I don't want that". "If I attract a mansion and yacht in the pacific, I might loose touch to my family". But even the deepest core-beliefs can be solved by recognizing the false dichotomies they are based on and replacing them with things such as: "I can have that mansion in the pacific *and* spend time with my family".

You can be, do and have anything within the terms defined prior to Incarnation. You do not have to wait until the afterlife to determine whether your life's goals are in alignment with your souls purpose or not. You can *feel* whether they are in sync. As a rule of the thumb: If something is strangely easy to experience, produce, create, attract, then it is in full alignment with what was determined pre-life. If something is in misalignment with that, you can still "get it", but it will take more work. This is why everyone on earth is working so hard: They have forgotten what it was they came here for. It is so much easier to just go with the stream of what you have chosen as a soul. Its so much easier flowing with what Higher Self has designed for you. Knowing that you have chosen the *general* path of your life you can ask yourself the following question when a big problem comes up:

"How does this serve me?"

And by labelling it as something that serves you in a positive way (no matter how bad it looks) it will turn out exactly that way for you. Once you recognize the positive benefit (from a soul plane perspective there is no such thing as "negative") the lesson is already learned and you can move on.

It was you, yourself, that has built in some traps and difficulties in life. And its beautiful to overcome them and remember that in the afterlife. I recall once traveling to Mongolia, cursing myself with "Why did I choose such an idiotic and burdening trip?". But in retrospect I will never forget the trip and the experience gave me more strength than I will ever need. As a child you did you want to celebrate Christmas by your parents buying a surprise that couldn't be seen until Christmas or did you want to celebrate it by just going into the store and grabbing it without wrapping or anything? What is more exciting? If the soul did not deliberately put limitations in place it would immediately have, do, be everything, without gift wrapping, without surprise. What many deem "enlightenment" or "being a millionaire" is actually one of the most boring things that could happen. No soul wants any of that because it's already been there a thousand of times. What the soul wants is to have nothing and be born into an unsafe and difficult environment and then from there acquire it all again.

After some time spent in the "Room of Choice", the soul makes its final decision and then retreats back to the group. Sometimes it prepares meticulously for its next life, sometimes it doesn't prepare at all and instead just hangs out with it's friends. Another factor that will limit your choice of Incarnations is that you will want to incarnate with some of your friends and will have to choose your incarnation in alignment with theirs. Your

Soul-Guide and the Choice-Room-Operator need to be quite on the ball to synchronize all of these factors. But its not necessary to pre-arrange that soulmates be born into the same family or town. You find them by natural attraction, even if you are thousands of miles apart.

My own physical parents actually frequented two of the location on a remote part of the globe at the same time years before they "officially met" (!). It was only years later the realized they were at the same place on the same day, long before having met. Usually we meet a similar group of people from life to life; our soul group members. With progress the group gradually changes. The Soul-Guide is the being you are in touch with the longest. Second in place are your soul mates and third your soul friends (members of the same overall exploration group). In some lives you make new soul friends. Some of them may become soul mates someday. In fourth place are people close to your exploration group. These are people you meet once in awhile during life, but they are not close to you. Sometimes a soul friend of yours will incarnate as one of your enemies or competitors. This is actually a favoured game. So if you do have any enemies or unwanted competitors, do take a closer look at them and ask yourself if they are more familiar to you than you'd like to admit. Sometimes we see two enemies becoming friends and feeling a great sense of novelty around it. In such a case you can be sure they played out the soul-friends-as-enemies game.

If you happen to meet many different type of groups and people throughout your life this is indicative of your soul being on a more advanced level. As my level is blue I have been in close contact to many thousands of people within my seminars and within the various organizations I am a member of. This is typical of my level. Typical for the violet level is to also be in touch with or influence many thousands of people...but without getting close to them. Pure white beginner souls on the other hand, will tend to meet very few people throughout their life and feel the best within the retrieve of their earthly family.

Incarnation goes more smoothly than death. While a child rests in its mothers womb the soul is able to merge with the child but also to leave again and roam around. It is only at around the age of three (!) that the soul stabilizes and begins to fully identify with the body and remain in its sphere most of the time (except when the body and mind are asleep). At the age of 6 the soul has voluntarily given up half of its ability to leave the body.

Merging with the body-mind (the body-mind has its own type of consciousness and energy-field) takes a few months. The soul examines the body, the nerve tracts, the brain and "makes friends" with them. With bodies and souls that are not a good match, the merging takes a bit longer. In rare cases the body "rebels" against the "invader" (soul energy), while others have no adaption issues at all. Most souls find it boring to stay near a body for 9 months and who travel around earth while the body is in the mothers womb, only visiting the body sporadically. It can only start with the adapting and merging process after the third month of pregnancy anyway and most souls start with the 6th or 7th month. Roaming around earths sphere before birth is one of the happiest days and adventures of a soul. This is one of only opportunities where the soul is able to travel the planet "out of body" in a carefree and untroubled manner. Souls that travel in and out of the body frequently before birth are more inclined to have "out of body experiences" during their later adult life.

Birth is not that big of a shock for the soul, but more of a shock for the body-mind. The general ambiance of hospitals on earth is in dire need of improvement. Crude glaring lights, frosty cold and nervous doctors are not the best welcome to the newly born. Ideally the light should be damped, the temperature pleasantly warm and the doctors relaxed but focused. As the soul is completely connected to the body for the event of birth, some of the bodies shock brushes off on it.

In the first years of the child, perception is not yet as strongly focused on earthly life. It fluctuates between the soul plane and the earth plane. That's why it is not uncommon for children to perceive and experience things that their parents do not perceive. They are able to see energy (such as other souls) which they label as "friends" and that parents stupidly label as "imaginary friends". Although the memory its existence on other planes and in other levels is already beginning to fade with birth, babies and children still have a little more "contact to the other side" (By the time they are able to communicate about it coherently, most of it is already gone). The way in which we underrate children is on one hand part of the game, but on the other hand pure ignorance. It's laughable, really. Those who later feel attracted to spiritual issues have never quite broken the connection to the other side, have never fully focused on the three dimensional planet earth. Today more and more souls are being born that no longer require 100% amnesia or suffering. Happier times are coming.

Techniques and Meditations

1. Recognizing people from the same soul group

This is fairly simple. It is the "inexplicable connection" you feel when meeting someone for the first time. "Seems familiar". "I just have the feeling that I know some things about this person although I have never met him". Sometimes the symbols, colors and professions connected to the person are the things reminding you of something. But essentially its a feeling. Whether you trust this feeling or not is up to you, but there is really no exercise or technique required here because all you have to pay attention to is what things are like the *first time* you meet this person...not later after all the layers and beliefs are put over the first impression.

Of which person would you like to know if he is part of your soul group or not? Think of that person right now. What did you feel the first time you met him/her? (If only indoctrinated "but I have to like him" thoughts come up, this is not the same thing as actually feeling something, by the way). Imagine never seeing this person again during your life. What comes up? Melancholy? Or the thought "Well, we will never really be separate". Both are obvious indicators that you are dealing with a soul friend. Now try this out with some of your relatives or even enemies.

2. Finding people from the same soul group

Now that you know the contents of this book you should have an easier time recognizing your soul friends. Some are part of your immediate surroundings, some you meet much later. And then there are those you should have met but missed, just like in the romantic soulmate movies. In order to attract your soul friends all you have to do is get into the correspondence-vibration of "friendship". Intend to meet "just the right people for me" and get into a state of appreciation for these people. And then watch out for what kind of people you meet in the three weeks thereafter.

3. Uncovering your Souls Intentions

Finding out what your soul originally intended before incarnating on this planet is your creative work that I cannot give you a specific technique for. You can get a sense of what your soul wants by looking at the talents you were given and the subjects that interest you most. You can look at what abilities come to you most easily and from that glean your souls intentions. Some Souls even define how you can access this type of Information during your lifetime. Most Souls give themselves some leeway and special keys with which they can create info leaks. I'd be the last person to know what exactly your unique methods are.

A general technique which may work for some, is to lie down and become silent. And as you lie there, to the best of your ability, produce a state of high Euphoria, all the while remaining calm and in lying position. The method you use to induce such a state is up to you (this should be natural Euphoria, not a state created by Drugs). Euphoria and Calm (which, in earth terms, are somewhat of a contradiction) best mirror the state you have on soul-plane. Therefore, producing that state puts you right in touch with your soul. Remain in that state without adding Imagination, Thought-Creation or Memory intentionally. Have the feeling but no intention to add mental images to it. Instead you wait for what mental images and thoughts come up by themselves, naturally, *as a response to the state you are in*. Simply witness what comes up, and whatever comes up can be something very different than what you expect or can even make sense of at first. Proceed in this way for about 5 to 10 Minutes and then immediately write down all the snippets and impressions you got, no matter what they were. Some of them will make sense right away, some of them may only make sense weeks or months later. Its important to write it all down. The images you *received* in that state are messages from the soul plane.

8

Lucid Dreaming

"He felt that his whole life was some kind of dream, and he sometimes wondered whose it was and if he was enjoying it".

- Douglas Adams

A lucid dream is a dream in which you know you are dreaming while you are dreaming. This level of awareness is not there in normal dreams. Lucid dreams are usually more vivid and enjoyable than regular dreams. Lucid dreamers do not practice conventional "dream interpretation" but dream *exploration*. In my experience, the ability allows for travel to exotic locations outside of earth, outside of our dimension, for telepathy (sharing a common dream with other dreamers), time-travel, remote viewing, healing, sports practice, influencing real life success, and many other exciting adventures.

The plane of night dreams is right between the physical and the non-physical. It is an intersection and a two-way-street to both. Dreams teach us a lot about how we create our reality because they show how consciousness projects worlds that the mind experiences as "real". When you are dreaming you are mostly convinced that something is taking place "out there". But when you wake up you realize it was a dream, you realize that it all took place *within*. Physical reality is no different than this self-created dream except in density and inertia. This means that things "manifest" more quickly and realities shift more fluidly within dreamscape, but that there is otherwise no difference between "dream" and "reality". It is our label of physical reality as "real" and "solid" and "meaningful" and our labelling of the dreamscape as "unreal" and "vague" and "insignificant" that makes most of the difference.

Lucid dreaming means to become *aware that you are dreaming while you are dreaming.* It is in this awareness that you suddenly realize you can change, stop, create or explore the dreamscape according to your own intention.

In dreams you access various life-streams, dimensions, planets, parallel universes. Extremely advanced practitioners could actually permit themselves to enter parallel universes with the result that their body disappears from this world. They will then be registered as a "missing person". I don't recommend this practice, I only mention it to hint at the magic that lies ahead.

Dreamscape is made up of realities that are not manifest, half-manifest and manifest – physically speaking. But even if a reality is "non-manifest" physically, that does not mean it has less intensity or reality to it. Seen from the souls perspective, non-physical reality is more real than the physical.

Learning Lucid Dreaming is not a requirement for spiritual growth. But it is an interesting field of study and a fun experience that can enhance your life. In fact, personally I am just content with LD itself, without having to understand, interpret or analyze it. When someone says to me he would like to make sense of his dreams I recommend him to enjoy the dreams instead. Afterall, you would not try to make sense of your experience while you are having sex or watching a good movie, would you? You would simply enjoy it. Trying to "make sense" of everything can be an impediment to enjoyment.

Learning it is simple: Become more *interested in and thereby more aware* of your dreaming. That is how you eventually become more aware *within* your dreaming. In the morning, right after waking, pay attention to what you dreamed and let the whole movie repeat in your head a few times. This is the key. Otherwise you forget it and its as if nothing ever happened. If you are more disciplined, you can also do this in writing. Write down everything you remember from your dream. Going through it a few times allows you to transfer it to waking memory. That is a very simple method of becoming more and more and more aware of your dream world. The only reason you would not do this is because you are not really interested in LD or think that dreams are not important. But they are. And as you become more aware of your dreams you will also, naturally become more aware that you are dreaming while you are dreaming.

If you have been using Visualization Techniques to attract a goal into your life, and the achievement of this goal appears in your nightdream, that is a sign that, in your current state of being, the goal is half-manifest. A reality can be 99% manifest before you see any of it in physical life. This is because physical reality only makes up 1% of your entire field of experience. The human "error" (or more precisely *game*) is to pretend the physical life is the only meaningful one. Getting in touch with the other realm means to take the world of thought, mind, emotion, dream more seriously. All of your "problems" come from the idea that the "inner realm" of thought and emotion is unimportant. Instead of seeing that the physical is a small part of reality you think the non-physical is a small part of reality. And unfortunately both old and modern schooling confirm this reversed view of things. Physical reality is only the tiniest outpost of all that is. Becoming aware of more is the same as becoming more. Taking life and physical reality too important leads to powerlessness

Lucid Dreaming also entails experiencing scenarios without having to experience them in waking life. *Before* something unpleasant manifests in "real life" you can confront it and turn it around in your dream. Of course you don't need the dream to do this, its just another option you have to make your life better. Or, you can live a secret desire that you don't quite allow to manifest in the physical. The reason you can experience the most fantastic and exhilarating things on dreamscape is because the mind, which acts as a reality-filter and censor, is asleep Its only the soul that is active here. The mind cant censor and the soul can do whatever it wants (or whatever has been suppressed by the waking-life mind). It would, however, be possible to allow many of these things to happen in physical reality if you release the censor just a little bit. The way reality behaves on dreamscape is the same way reality behaves in physical waking life, with the difference of physical being slower, more inert and of heavier vibration. In this way Lucid Dreaming is a practice or testing field for the creation of reality.

If we were to identify levels of dream awareness on a scale it might look something like this:

Scale of Dream Lucidity

1 Totally Unaware

After waking up you don't even remember you dreamed.

2 Unaware

Its only after waking up that you notice you dreamed. The "signs that I'm dreaming" only become obvious after its already over rather than during the dream. During the dream you don't question anything happening but just let it roll over you. If its a nightmare you feel quite helpless. But on this level you can at least recap the dream. The morning recap helps you rise to higher levels of dream awareness.

3 Semi-aware

While dreaming you do sense or realize that something is strange, but you don't question it. There might be tiny flickers of awareness on what meanings some aspects of the dreams have but you don't quite get around to acknowledging the dream as a dream. On this level you at least remember your dreams when you wake up.

4 Semi-lucid

In this pre-lucid state you notice that "something is going on" during the dream. Certain hints and indicators make you think you might be dreaming. You try to question it but never get quite lucid. Its as if one part of you, in the background, knows its a dream, but another part of you does not quite summon the energy to intervene or care. Sometimes the question "Is this a dream???" arises but is quickly forgotten in the mist of the dreamscape stimuli.

Sometimes we don't reach this level from the lower ones but descend to it from the higher levels. We were lucid before but then descend into semi-lucidity. One example of this is knowing that you are dreaming but then having a "false awakening". Now you believe you are awake, but you are still dreaming. This is one of the typical protection-systems installed to prevent "too much" awareness.

5 Lucid

Because of certain indicators or a heightened level of awareness or other triggers and circumstances, you become aware that you are dreaming (or you drift into the dream already aware of what it is). You recognize the dream *as* a dream. "Ah, interesting. I'm dreaming". On this level the realization and its accompanying feeling of lightness or curiosity is enjoyed like a movie rather than your dream-self getting actively involved.

6 Very Lucid

This is a state of pleasant clarity in which you understand what is happening even more obviously. Furthermore, you become aware that you can *influence* the dream. Possibilities for action and behavior, your own role and mission within the dream become more apparent. This is the lucid dreamer who can actually *fully* enjoy the dream.

7 Luminously Lucid

This is crystal clear lucidity and well-being which sometimes tips over into euphoria and various states of bliss. Here you take active control of the dream or, alternatively just let it play out and enjoy it. This is the realm in which you can use the dream to explore various dimensions of existence, act creatively, or apply therapeutic measures to your waking-life-self.

8 Illuminatingly Lucid

Awareness of different meanings and layers of what you are currently experiencing. On this level you not only know that you can do whatever you want, but also which tasks you are here to fulfil Intuitive guidance, communication with other beings, recognition of long-term solutions or healing and states of pure bliss are common here.

Don't take this scale as "gospel". Its a general outline for contrast and comparison. Rather than going too much into what can be done with lucid dreaming or what I've done with it, I would now like to support you in "getting into it". I trust that if you actually "get into it" you will find out the different practical uses and/or entertainment options yourself.

Inducing Lucid Dreams

Generally, every type of desired reality, including lucid dreaming, comes about by investing interest into it. So rather than having the "future goal" of "someday" lucid dreaming, you just get into the flow of interest right away. And what if you are not willing to invest interest? Then don't. But don't be pretending you are going to lucid dream then. It is the *interest* itself that will produce lucid dreams and it doesn't take that much effort. Some people lucid dream only due to having talked about the subject to someone during the day. Believing that you need all kinds of practice and technique before you can enjoy this natural ability is a lie that will stifle your progress. Be interested. *Let it* happen.

There are many ways to demonstrate your interest to your conscious mind, subconscious mind or whichever part of you has the final say. One is, as mentioned, to repeat the dream movie in the morning, right after waking up. Commit it to memory. Did you know that you literally *assemble* the world in the morning? Without consciousness, without an observer, there is no reality. This *assembling* of reality happens at such a quick speed that it is hardly noticed. People wake up and think "OK, here I am, back in the world", without noticing that they assembled their surroundings according to their innermost expectations. This is why it is important how you wake up in the morning and how you start the day. I recommend starting it with a time-out. Instead of falling into the habitual pattern of thinking a thousand thoughts about life, the world, the day, the people, you can call out a "stop" and just lie there and observe. Or replay your dreams. *As you become aware of dream-life during waking life, you become aware of waking life during dream life. Lucid dreaming is nothing more than being aware that there is "another reality" "out there" called "waking life".* There is not only one reality, the dream you are facing, but another one.

A benefit of actually writing a Dream-Journal in the morning is that Dreams contain hints. Hints on where to go, what to purchase, things to do. Sometimes you are even given hints of what to do in order to increase your lucid-dreaming. If your soul tells you "sleep with a headband or hat", then it doesn't matter how silly this advice appears to the mind. Do it. As only the soul is active on dreamscape and the mind is asleep, the *quality of advice given is much higher* than that of your waking self. The souls advice is always for your benefit.

Another Lucid Dream inducer is to not sleep as deeply as you are used to. A common block to lucid dreaming is being so exhausted during waking life that your night is spent in sleep so deep and "wiped out" that you are far from any sort of sleep awareness. This is why leading a conscious and healthy life naturally improves dream life. If your day is full of unawareness and resistance don't expect your night to be any different. For not sleeping as deeply, lucid dreamers have suggested a number of things. One is to listen to audio recordings (guided Meditations, Music, LD Inductions) before going to sleep. Some practice unusual yogic postures while sleeping. Others hold heavy weights that will fall down and wake them up if they drift too far off into sleep. Others use caffeine. Vitamin B6 and melatonin or heavy foods are taken so that the body stays active and the mind therefore half-aware. Often sleeping in new or unfamiliar locations will induce dream awareness.

Some fall into a Lucid Dream while falling asleep, others "wake up in" a lucid dream while already asleep. The method of falling into a lucid dream is more common and easier for practitioners. Waking up within a Dream is mostly seen as unintentional. One way to fall into a lucid dream is by talking to yourself while you slowly drift into sleep. Once you are unable to move your mouth because your body is sleeping, you continue talking to yourself in your mind. Or, if you prefer visioning instead of talking, you can loose yourself in pleasant imagery while falling asleep but catching yourself every time you fall too deep. This is more difficult and requires some practice.

There is a state between waking and sleeping called "hypnagogic state" in which all kinds of muddled and confusing and sometimes quite trashy mind-material are processed. Once you have reached the hypnagogic state its almost too late to "drift into a lucid dream" because you've already lost most of your awareness. Focusing on pleasant imagery while falling asleep or listening to a positive recording will not only help you lucid dream but also make both your dream and your state of mind the next morning more positive. Add the clear intention to stay awake and aware to your exercise. Say: "I allow my whole body to fall asleep but my mind to stay awake and aware". Keep making the decision to fall asleep while a part of you remains alert. <

When practicing "guided imagery" while falling asleep, it can be wise to *emulate* things you would be doing if you were lucid. Being lucid means that one can *change, create, stop, reverse* things. The same can be done in your visualization. In other words: Lucid dream before you lucid dream! Whatever it is you wish to experience as a lucid dreamer, do it in your imagination. Teach your body-mind what it is like to lucid dream. This will make the actual event more likely to happen. Lets say you are visualizing a pyramid. Well then...place it somewhere else. Change its color. Change its size and shape. Examine it from all sides. Make it disappear. Make it appear again. Go inside it. Exercise and get a handle over the imagined dreamscape.

Do you see why lucid dreaming can be somewhat tricky? Its contradictory: On the one hand you can only experience it if you fall asleep, on the other hand you can only experience it if a part of you stays awake. *Falling asleep while staying awake* produces extraordinary lucid dreams.

Another technique proposed by Lucid Dreamers out there is to frequently question yourself and your surroundings. They call this "reality-tests".

"Am I dreaming?"

"Is this a dream?"

"Is this real?"

"What's really going on here?".

By getting used to questioning what is happening in waking-life, the habit rubs off on the dream-state and you may find yourself asking "Am I dreaming?" - and thereby become lucid. This seems to work even better when unusual events occur in the waking state. Something strange happens and you say "Is this a dream?". The reason for this is that we often become lucid in night dreams because of some weirdness or out-of-place event or out-of-place object. "This isn't for real, is it?" Its the strangeness that prompts the dreamer to question it. Therefore Lucid Dreamers often walk around in *waking life* asking "Am I dreaming" and even answering "Yes, this is a dream" or "Yes, I am dreaming!". What I have also noticed is that in life phases in which you are more lucid or more in touch with your dreams more of this strangeness may occur. I once woke up one early morning feeling rather lucid after quite the vivid dream. I went out on my balcony for a breathe of fresh air. The air was morning crisp and smelled of autumn/fall. The sun was shining but the streets and trees were wet from recent rainfall. There were no cars or people to be seen anywhere. It was Sunday morning. Then suddenly, out of the blue, came some kind of strange car-like contraption. I had never seen anything like it. It had only three wills and was electrically powered. An old lady was sitting in it, but the driving-device looked super-futuristic, like something out of a far-future-sci-fi movie. It glittered and sparkled in the sun as it drove by. I had seen three-wheelers and also electric cars before but I had never seen anything odd like this. And so I took the opportunity to ask myself: "Am I dreaming?" "Is this for real?". It is quite possible that I only experienced this moment of oddity because I was in a slightly altered state to begin with. We do experience our world and its events according to our state. As if to confirm this, on the very same day I received an odd email. It was as if the email was sent out of some alternate universe. Someone I had had a crush on in High School was writing to me – although she completely disregarded me back then. How often does that happen? Hardly ever. So on that particular day I was certainly in a different zone than I normally am. Finally, in the evening, I was driving down a road, heading home. I was driving through a wooded section. I could see someone standing at the side of the road, hitchhiking. That's unusual enough because I had never seen anyone hitchhike in the area, much less in such thick woods far away from any village. When I started to make out the persons face, I sped up quickly indeed. One could say I was spooked out.. It was a lady that looked like the long lost girl I had received an email from earlier. Later I stopped at a gas-station. I had stopped here many, many times. Never before has there been nobody behind the counter. And nobody was there for a record time of 15 Minutes. In the area I lived that was unthinkable. The clerk just said "I'm sorry, I was in the restroom". So this is how a day in lucid-state goes. You know you are in that zone when things happen that have never happened before. Literally out-of-the-ordinary. Or when things go exactly like they usually do, but with a little edge, with a little oddity or just slightly misplaced.

If your using the more advanced method of waking up within a dream, one way of doing this would be to condition yourself to look for a light-switch in the dream. What happens when you try turning on a light-switch in a dream? Have you ever been in the dark and afraid the light-switch wont work? This fear may be connected to a strange anomaly often encountered in lucid dreams: That it is difficult to turn on the light or to operate light-switches. What could the reason for this be? I don't know. Maybe it's because of time-anomalies connected to light. As time moves differently on dreamscape we'd perhaps become "too aware" of that. Or maybe it's because sub-awareness levels don't wish to be illuminated. Or (my personal theory) it's connected to the fact that there is no such thing as darkness but only light (darkness not being a thing itself but only an absence of light), which eliminates the necessity of turning light on or off. In any case, looking for a light-switch or trying to turn on a light is a good reality-test for within a dream (if you can remember to do reality-tests within a dream). If you have intended to fulfil a certain task in waking life and actually remember intending that, you automatically become lucid. Any remembrance of things in waking life ("there's another reality out there!") will make you lucid. Another reality-test some use within a dream is to try calculating, counting your using maths. If you find yourself unable to fulfil the most basic math exercises (What is 20 minus 10?) then you can be sure you're dreaming. The fluid nature of dreamscape reveals itself anytime you try to focus or read something. Intellectual exercises that involve numbers and writing are extremely difficult on dreamscape because the part of your mind responsible for analysis is turned off. If it weren't, you could not lucid dream, because analysis means to filter energy. Another "reality-test" some conduct during dreams is to turn around their own axis very quickly and then abruptly stop. This "spinning" reveals that your environment will keep turning after you've stopped because it has to assemble itself again. In this way you are shown that your surroundings are a reflection of your consciousness rather than there being any dreamscape outside and independent of you. The same applies to physical life, but in a much slower way: Change yourself and your surroundings reassemble to reflect that change.

The question "Where was I just now" is another popular one with Lucid Dreamers. In waking and sleeping. If you're on some ship heading towards an island outside of Canada and you ask "Where was I just now?" or "Where was I before this?" and you realize that you were in a Cafe in India - you know you are dreaming. Linear-time and space reality on earth does not work that way. Before you are in India you have to be at some airport in Canada, and then in some plane and then at some stopover perhaps. Earth-reality is linear. Yet another reality-test is to question "false awakening". While all this requires awareness to begin with, it also facilitates awareness to "test-drive" these things in waking life and in your imagination. "False-awakening" is a frequent trick played on yourself to fall from lucid to non-lucid. Its a sort of "back-up-program" of your sub-aware levels that seek to "protect" you from "flying too high". Therefore, the reality-test upon awakening is to ask "Have I really awoken or am I still, in fact, dreaming?". Taken to the extreme you might want to hang up signs all over your living space with the question "Am I dreaming?"

A list of other indicators that you are dreaming (think about these before falling asleep if you want. Recognizing a dream as a dream induces lucid dreaming!):

New places

New faces

Frustrating or unsolvable tasks

Everything unexpected, different and strange

Inconsistent passage of time or space

Living in a new house

Living with another person

Having another profession

Back at school

Meeting people from the past

Fantasy and science-fiction scenarios

Meeting new people

Paranormal activity

Intense beauty

Looming danger, fight or escape

Flying

Floating into the air (often accompanied by respective body movements)

Problems moving

Problems with orientation

You look different

Loss of body control

Non-logical events and sequences

Surprising sexual activity

and more...

We often loose ourselves in a dream like we loose ourselves in a book or good movie. Since we are participating in the dream, it is easy to forget that we are dreaming or to take on the observer-mode of the lucid dreamer. More of a neutral stance (less emotionally involved) can be helpful for beginners. "Reality-tests" during moments of emotional upheaval in daily life are especially helpful, not only for lucid dreaming but for living a more conscious life in general.

Imagine what it would feel like to suddenly realize that you are dreaming. Do this right now. Intensify this thinking to a point where you feel shivers run down your spine. "Oh my God! Its all a dream!" Nothing that you currently perceive in your surroundings is solid or real, nothing represents "ultimate reality". Your real self is safely waiting elsewhere for your return from this dream world. Nothing you do has adverse consequences. Try simulating this impression for a few minutes. Look around at the dream scenario. *In a sense* this is true. After you die and leave this planet you will, in a sense "wake up" to a "more real" self; the one you were before entering this dream. (This does not mean that suicide is advisable. Deliberately cutting yourself off from the originally intended stream of things has dire consequences, one of which is becoming an "earthbound spirit"). Look around in the awareness that its all a dream. And with that realization you may feel some relief. In any case, becoming lucid during a night dream causes relief because you know you are no longer the victim of circumstances but can create better. "Awakening" in your sleep corresponds to little "awakenings" in your waking life. Being able to do one, influences your ability to do the other. Both universes – waking and dreaming – reflect each other.

The more extreme version of reality-testing I came up with myself. I call it "reality breaking". This is where you create the weirdness or radical routine-break yourself. This would be any action that would cause someone to say "I must be dreaming!" It means doing something unexpected, sudden, very different. It means breaking with current reality. The vibrational-signal you send out when doing this is: "Reality is not what it was up to now. Reality is what I create it to be! I decide!". Reality Breaking is a form of ending the daily hypnosis we are often in and is, of course, also useful apart from purposes of LD.. Reality Breaking can mean to suddenly walk backwards. When I was younger, before I owned a car, there was a stretch I had to walk every day. And I tried walking this stretch differently everyday. Once I walked the whole stretch backwards. At another time I walked the whole stretch while looking at the clouds. Another time the whole stretch was seen by looking into the distance only. I did this to break by habitual viewing. It can mean to wash your face with champagne instead of drinking it. To speak to someone you have never spoken to before. To react to a problem by being overjoyed. By taking your laptop and all other hardware you own for a ride in the car. If that strangeness transfers to sleeping life you will not only be able to turn a normal dream into a waking dream but even break or transform nightmares. If you are being followed by a monster and suddenly do something that is completely out-of-script, the monster looses control. The monster is revealed as part of a movie *you have scripted*. By doing something out of line with an automatic script, you tear the filmstrip and regain control.

Another technique – one of the most useful - is to set the alarm clock for unusual times and then fall back to sleep. This is done as to not fall asleep too deeply, to remain in that space in which there is still some awareness. The best times to set on the alarm clock seem to be in morning hours between 3 and 9 a.m. Some of the best lucid dreams occur in the morning. The light from outside and the morning sounds and noises serve to activate some awareness (the fact that we register external sound while sleeping proves that we never really "loose awareness" as some claim).

What I sometimes use is brainwave entrainment music which I set on auto-play or auto-repeat so that it continues to play while I sleep. For this you can use any of the binaural or hemisphere synchronization music on the market or you can use my Audios on Lucid Dreaming (which you will find in the "Guided Meditations" Section of www.realitycreation.net). Using my "Lucid Dream Creator" for example, will train your awareness to remain awake so that you eventually do slip into a Lucid Dream.

Another technique some Dreamers use is "getting back into the dream". After waking up you memorize where you've been (the dream) and fall back asleep with the intention to re-experience that. Sometimes we do this anyway when awoken from a nice dream. "I want to go back and continue the dream!". Because we are moving back in deliberately often full lucidity is produced. Similar can be said of "continuing the dream of last night".

There are only three states of consciousness: Waking, dreaming and deep sleep. By being a bit more aware of what happens during the *transitions* from and to these three states crossover and spillover is more likely to occur. In life-phases that I wish to re-activate my lucid dream abilities I usually not only remember my dream in the morning but repeat the memory throughout the day and then remember the same dream again while falling asleep. This is an easier path to lucid dreaming than "becoming aware of the exact moment you fall asleep".

Wake up more softly. Loud and sudden awakenings with a shrill alarm clock can cause dream-amnesia. Likewise a partner that is excessively loud in the morning. These mini-traumas can cause the impression that you did not dream at all. Gently ask your partner to tone it down in the morning. It may be necessary to gently ask him or her repeatedly, until the new idea sticks to their memory. Do not say "Don't be so loud!" because then you are programming what you don't want – loudness. If you really believe you need an alarm clock for reasons of profession or otherwise, then see if you can get one that is more soothing. Chirping birds, a flowing stream or a piano playing will do. If you are now saying "I cant wake up to that!" then you are too exhausted to be practicing lucid dreaming anyway and ought to find a way to lead a more refreshing life.

You can bypass all of these exercise if your intention is strong and convincing. Proper "intending" is done without expectation, desire or need but only with certainty. Intend to stand up. Now stand up. See? There was no doubt whatsoever about standing up and that's what happened. This is the proper use of intent. Your intent should be repeated over days and weeks to remind yourself of what it is you are doing at night. Also consider voicing your intent in the past-tense, as if its already happened. "I had a good lucid dream last night" When you did have a lucid dream, be grateful for it. Remember it. Emphasize it. Talk about it. Tell someone about it. If you had a lucid dream and don't really care, your soul will not be as forthcoming in delivering another one.

Any act of awareness or any intentional act connected with pre-sleep is helpful because lucid dreaming is all about not completely loosing awareness. You may meditate or apply breathing techniques or reality-tests or Meditation. The paradox is that you do too much of this stuff you'll have too much energy to fall asleep and will lie awake in bed instead of dreaming! You are therefore looking for the right balance between sleepiness and wakefulness.

A "strange" part of lucidity is that during dreams we often remember other dreams we had. But this is not actually that strange since we only remember according to the state we are in, according to who we are. Once you are back in a certain state you remember the things you experienced the last time you were in that state. Its a fun and surprising realization to notice that your "dream-self" has a completely different memory-cache than your waking-self. This special function can be used to intensify your dream-awareness. When the opportunity arises to remember other dreams during the dream state, seize that opportunity and re-member, re-integrate, re-intensify.

Lucid Meditations

These Meditations can induce states of lucidity, no matter if you are waking or dreaming. As already mentioned, your waking life is a dream too and you often behave in an unaware way, as if life were real. No matter if you increase your lucidity during sleep or in waking, one will effect the other.

Intensifying Attention

Examine any object in detail until you "loose yourself" in it. Become aware of details you hadn't noticed before. You know you've lost yourself within the object once you forget your daily life, time, space, your surroundings, urgencies and anything else. After you've lost yourself in that "reality" to a certain extent, "wake yourself up" again by releasing attention and looking around. Repeat this a few times. This can also be done with thoughtforms. Both, intensifying attention and the release of attention are valuable psychospiritual abilities.

Intensifying Awareness

Look at something. But while looking at it remain aware of other things outside of the periphery of your view. All you're doing here is focusing something while remaining aware of other things. Focus without fixing to something. So you might be looking at a car but at the same time remain aware of the tree at the border of your vision and the other cars outside of your field of vision. This can be done with objects, thoughts and even with people (while they talk to you, you remain aware of other things and do not become hypnotized by the person).

Finally, try to remain aware of everything in your surroundings, do not fix on anything.. Sit there for awhile and be Awareness itself.

Intensifying your Senses

a) Focus your entire awareness and senses on something physical in waking reality while thinking about focusing on the same thing during your sleeping reality.

b) While falling asleep, recall and re-experience that quality or reality mentally. Intend to re-experience it a third time during your sleep.

Example: a) You eat real, physical ice-cream and sensually enjoy it, while thinking about experiencing the same thing during your sleep. b) You re-experience eating that ice-cream mentally while thinking about experiencing the same thing during your sleep. c) you will experience that during your sleep.

9

Awareness

This chapter teaches how to increase your Awareness so that you can "wear life like a light garment" more in sync with the reality and energy-level of the soul. The articles contained herein were first published on my Blog at realitycreation.org

From Thinking to Feeling

Life is energy and that energy always flows. If you are resisting that flow of energy, your breathing becomes more shallow, your muscles become more contracted and you are more into *thinking* and *wanting*. If you go with that flow of energy, your breathing becomes slower and softer, your muscles are relaxed and you are more into *feeling* and *being*.

Letting more and more go of thinking or of looking in the mind for answers will not reduce your Intelligence or make you dull. The mind is useful for many things of daily life, but it does not know happiness and energy, just like a Computer couldn't be happy. Letting go of seeking answers, trying to understand things, trying to grasp everything with the intellect will actually make you smarter. Don't you notice how the more someone applies exertion and tightens his forehead in an attempt to figure things out, the stupider he gets? Its a misconception that a lot of thinking gets things done or solves issues. Even scientific discoveries and research are best done in a mix of thinking and receiving, of mind and emptiness, of concentration and release.

Reducing your thinking will increase your power and happiness. But trying to get rid of or suppress thinking will not work. What will work is feeling. When you notice yourself get tense, unwell or into too much thinking and wanting (wanting = lack. Thinking-ness and Wanting-ness always appear together), simply return back to feeling. Return back to energy. The quickest way to do this is to re-direct your attention into your body. This is also called "getting out of the head". So rather than being preoccupied with the mind and having attention in the head-area (consciousness loves hanging around in the head area), you redirect your attention to your stomach or chest or arms or legs or simply to feeling. Feeling what? Just feeling whatever is there. Whatever you are feeling right now. The mind will say that you are "supposed to" feel this or that way, but that's just the minds commentary. The mind always provides commentary. You cant stop the mind. Meditators try to stop it, but that's impossible.. Just let the TV Set run, its not important. When going to your feelings, letting your feelings be your guide, the most important thing is to stop resisting feeling itself. The way you have been brought up as a human being there is a 90% of you resisting what you are feeling this moment.

So take a deep breathe and just feel what you are feeling right now. Feel your life energy right now. When you feel life, you feel all the energy passing through, without filters. Thinking-ness is like putting filters on that energy. After awhile you only perceive a tiny percentage of all the energy.

Sit in an upright position. Watch your breathing. Do this for a minute or two.

Notice how just watching your breathing clears the mind and lifts your mood.

Breathing is connected to feeling. Cutting off the breathe of life is connected to thinking.

The mind is essentially a recording machine. It records information and then it plays that information again and again. This can be very useful to draw upon a large amount of information and align your intentions and actions. But it can also become a burden when you keep playing the same old negative records over and over. The funny thing is that it thinks its helping and protecting you by playing negative records over and over. The reasoning goes: "If you are afraid of this, you are protected from it". In reality just the opposite is true. Fear does not protect you from what is feared, it attracts what is feared. If you wish to empower yourself you'll have to overcome this basic mistake that is implanted within each and every human like some kind of programming error. All type of attention on the problem does not solve it. So let go of trying to solve it, grasp it, understand it, figure it out...and return to feeling. What will then happen is that it will solve itself.

Return to resistance-less feeling every time you notice yourself get back into thinking, wanting and resistance.

Let all energies, emotions, feelings that come up just pass by and pass through. If you don't resist them, they just pass through. When something painful comes up, there is the tendency to stop that energy or try to push it back down. This does not get rid of the energy, it just puts it back into your subconscious. In this way you may not feel it anymore but you do not have a gain in energy but an overall loss. If you let that "painful" emotion come up and out it may be more painful then usual but in the long run there is a gain in calm, a gain in lightness, a gain in emotional clearing. People who practice this may be experiencing more emotional "pain" than other people because they are letting it come up and out. All other people keep it down in their subconscious. They will have to face it some day. But in reality there is no such thing as emotional "Pain". It only feels like pain if there is still a part of you pushing it. Just let it completely come up and out.

One basic practice is to feel into each body part before going to sleep. Have your attention be in your right foot. And then the left foot. And in this way gently through the whole body. If you practice this for awhile you will start feeling your energy and aliveness again. You may also effect the quality of your night-dreams positively.

Remember that 99% of real life is completely invisible. Its the energy all around. The mind is always preoccupied with the visible, with the 1%. If you wish to access the 99%, stop resisting life and instead feel it.

Start and Stop

Another way to increase awareness is by not having all of your movements and actions run on automatic but controlling some of them. A practice I've once seen Japanese Buddhists do is "extremely slow walking". Starting in the morning, they would walk 300 feet by evening. This amount of self-control seems impossible for most people. But even only taking 1% of that attitude can improve your life. Choose a day on which to do everything just a little more slowly. Down the stairs more slowly. Turn the ignition more slowly. Shower more slowly. Drive the car more slowly. See how it improves your overall state of Awareness. "Haste makes waste" is an old saying and always holds true. Haste is created by the ever needy and ever lacking Mind/Ego in an attempt to "gain" something it thinks is missing. But Spirit is never in a hurry. It is never under pressure. it is never lacking.

One variation of this is to deliberately start or stop something. Have you ever, while walking down a hallway at work, just stopped in your tracks, right there and then? If you're like most people, you probably haven't Why not? Because you're on automatic. You are running like a wind-up-toy according to what is expected of you or according to what everyone else does. When you stop in your tracks, you stop the Movie of life and fall into silence. From this stillness it is easier to determine what the Movie should be about. Otherwise the movie determines what your life is about. If you normally smoke after eating, why not just stop that today and not smoke after eating? Or if you normally never have a cup of tea after eating, why not just start today and always have tea after eating?

The easier it is for you to Stop and Start things, the more creative control you have over reality.

Stopping and Starting things may bring up various subconscious resistances. If so, that's OK. Let them pass by. If you never say hello to strangers, say hello today. If you always say hello to strangers, don't say it today. You can change the script your life goes by, at any time. And even small changes are helpful in that they introduce an element of choice and free will and deliberate action into your daily life.

Here's one of my favourite Meditation-Techniques to experience 100% Awareness for a few minutes. Say what you are going to do next and then do it. For a few minutes, don't do anything without deciding to beforehand. "I am going to walk over to that window" (do it). "I am going to touch that window" (do it). "I am going to sit down" (do it). 15 Minutes of this puts you back into a state of full control of your reality. I recommend the exercise for anyone who's life has become confusing, exhausting, overwhelming. The advanced version of the exercise is to watch out for automatic behaviours (during the exercise), and to step back and do these behaviours intentionally. So if I say "I am going to the window" and I brush through my hair while going there, I would stop and say: "I am going to brush through my hair" (do it) and then again: ""I am going to go to the window".

You will notice that most things in your life run on automatic. That is not a problem. You don't need to do everything intentionally. Its fine if the hundreds of movements required to drive a car go on automatic. The problems come up when **too much** of your life is running on automatic. Then every day is the same as the day before: Get up. Wash. Drive. Sit in office cubicle. Drive. Watch TV. Sleep.

Having just a little bit more self-control will help you be both more calm and also more productive. You will make better decisions in life because you are coming from a place of clarity, not from the rat-race people call "normal life".

You are able to stop talking when you like and start talking when you like. To stop biting your nails and to start. To stop drinking coffee and to start.

Love is to give Attention, Time and Space

Love is the primary lesson of this life on this planet. All other lessons are secondary to that. If you have solved the Love issue, you have automatically solved all other issues. Where there is lack...any lack at all...lack of health, friends, money, joy...there was always lack of Love there first.

When I say to students "give yourself love" or "love

yourself", what does that really mean? It means to give yourself attention, time, space. The old English word for fear is *angst*. This word comes from the Germanic *eng*, which means tight, narrow or contracted.. Any time a tightness arises it is because you are not giving yourself time, space or attention.

When a client of yours starts complaining, its because you have not given that client Love. Give that client either more time, or more attention or more space, and they will stop complaining.

When a spouse starts becoming a stranger to you, its time to give Love. Spend more time with them. Or, if you think you don't have time, then give more attention in the little time you do spend. Or, if you don't have attention either, give your spouse the space to say, do and be whatever they want. If you have neither time, attention nor space, start relaxing, opening up and regaining Awareness.

If your body is feeling unwell, open up and give your body more love. Sit or lie many ours with your body only. That's the whole purpose of going to bed when you fall ill. Going to bed gives you the opportunity to send love and appreciation to your body.

If you lack income, open up and send more love to yourself, others and the world. Release your resentment of rich people, your resentment of success, your resentment toward working, your resentment of everything. Give the issue some time, space and attention.

Giving Space: Allowing things to unfold naturally. Allowing others to be who they are, without trying to change or control them. Allowing life to unfold naturally.

Giving Attention: Looking at, Listening to, Thinking about something or someone. Being with someone or something, without constant preoccupation with yourself or your own "issues".

Giving Time: Spending an amount of time with someone or something. Patiently resting with someone or something. Enjoying time spent with someone or something without restlessly going to and fro.

Pleasure Delay

Most children are not able to delay gratification. If you offer them a small candy bar now or a bigger one later, most of them will choose the smaller. This tendency to want immediate and instant results and gratification lessens with maturity. Unfortunately some adults still display it. I recently watched a grown man pay $700 more for a gadget because he couldn't wait for a week when that gadget was expected to be reduced in price by 50%,.

I frequently refer to "being source". "Being source" means being cause of your attention and emotions rather than letting the world play you like a ball. If you are source of your energy, you don't desperately "need" anything. You have no problem delaying so-called "pleasures". In fact, since you know that all happiness comes from within, nobody can control or lure you with all of these supposed "pleasures". Does this mean you no longer strive for pleasures? No, it means you are no longer slave to them. And because you are no longer slave to them you enjoy them so much more than someone constantly seeking instant gratification.

Do not turn your spiritual journey into seeking ultimate or rapid results but into a long-term lifestyle of growth, appreciation and constant learning. There is no "ultimate goal" to "reach". If there were, you would immediately stop learning and stop growing. All challenges are fantastic opportunities to grow. Opportunities to embrace whatever comes up.

Replace Gratification with Gratitude.. Seeking gratification is what makes you weak. Gratitude makes you powerful. Seeking gratification implies lack. Giving Gratitude implies abundance.

There are many ways to implement this lesson into your life. You don't have to have Sex on your first date, not even on the second. Its so much more intense if you can delay it for a bit. You don't have to have chocolate right now, you can have some later. How about experimenting and trying to have chocolate when you don't want any and not having some when you want some. This breaks your conditioning a little and puts you back into being Source of your Reality rather than Victim of your cravings.

The 3 heads of the world-self

...are the chicken, the pig and the snake.

The chicken is the restless energy, pecking around here

and there, never focused, always moving, pecking even if there is nothing to peck. This head runs rampant in society where the attention of the average human shifts from one thing to the next, reading hundreds of news items but not going more deeply into any one subject, following this, that and that but not learning anything, trying this, this and that but not mastering anything. The chicken-energy of the world-self can be transcended through slowing down, focussing attention, deliberate-non-doing throughout the day, meditation, etc.

The pig energy is a heavy energy that is primarily concerned with indulging in food and sex. And after its desires are fulfilled it is stuffed and complacent. This head runs rampant in our society where the attention of the average human is hardly interested in spiritual matters but in the quick fulfilment of supposed "needs". The content of earth becomes more important than its context. The main point of having dinner with others is then not to join the person and exchange information and energy, but to eat. The main point of making love to another is then not to join the person and exchange love and energy, but to gratify an addiction. The pig-energy of the world-self can be transcended through discipline, poise, deliberate-doing, meditation, etc.

The snake energy is a cold-blooded, vicious energy that is primarily concerned with mindless and heartless Attack and Domination. This head runs rampant in our society where the attention of the average human has no interest or concern whatsoever for anything but its small little self and its small little world. The snake energy is void of compassion or understanding. Everything that it encounters it's trying to calculate an advantage for itself. "What can I get out of it?". If someone crosses it in highway traffic it literally wants to kill that person, it wants to rip off the persons neck. The snake-energy of the world-self can be transcended through Relaxation, Appreciation, Compassion, Love of oneself, others and the world.

Being too concerned about yourself is a limitation. If you release your concern about your Reputation or how you look toward others, or whether you will succeed, or what others think about your work, you gain freedom, power, creativity and productivity. Why? Because your attention is no longer stuck on a small sphere around your own head, no longer stuck on worry. No longer strongly identified with "I" and "me, me, me" your sphere of influence expands to things "outside of yourself".

"Paradoxically" the more concerned you are about yourself and your influence, the less you have. A few small exercise that will expand your sphere-of-influence and perception and help you get out of identifying with that tiny body and head you call "me":

* While taking a walk, notice when you are preoccupied with thinking. Release that tendency and instead shift your awareness to your surroundings, the objects, plants and people in your surroundings. Become interested in the World. Every time you have a relapse into Thinking, return to extroverting your attention again.

* Anonymously make someone a gift

* Genuinely forgive and then publicly praise someone you held a grudge against

* Spontaneously give up trying to solve something you've been thinking about for a long time and just forget about it.

Enjoy the Expansion.

Duality, Control and Surrender

Some teach Control as a means of success in life. They say you have to be disciplined, focus, control yourself (and in this way control circumstances), take action, set priorities, reach goals, etc. Others teach Surrender as a means of success in life. They say you have to let go, release, let it flow, allow the Universe to take over, give up all effort and struggle.

Mine is one of the few "schools of thought" that teaches both. If you only surrender all the time you don't train your will and determination. If you only control all the time you don't allow the Universe to work greater miracles than you'd be capable of. The art of living is knowing when to control and when to surrender. When to act and when to relax. When to fight and when to forgive. An Aware person then, is neither a control-freak who needs to dominate and prove his will all the time, nor a pansy who passively sits back and turns the other cheek all the time. He is balanced and recognizes both his own will and divine will.

The same applies to all other Dualities. Being an Aware

Person, you become both expert at Non-Doing, as well as Doing. If you can fully embrace one side of the coin, you can fully embrace the other. Notice how people who don't feel good about hard work, don't feel good about total relaxation either. They might pretend they do but deep down they feel guilty about letting it all hang loose and being lazy. And so they are stuck in a realm of neither-nor. They don't want to work and they don't want to not-work.

A soul loves to work. And a soul loves to be lazy. A soul loves being together with someone. A soul loves being alone. Neither side of the duality poses a problem. A soul loves being rich. A soul loves being poor. The Ego loves neither. The Ego always dislikes both sides, the soul always likes both sides. For the Ego the room is too warm or its too cool. From the perspective of Higher Self, everything unfolding perfectly as it is.

If you wish to master any subject in life, just practice loving both sides. if you want to master calm, then master both tension and calm. If you want to master prosperity, master both prosperity and poverty. If you want to master fear, master both fear and courage. All issues come in pairs of two but we often only recognize one side of the coin...and therefore only live half of our potential. If you remember only one thing from reading this article, let it be: Every issue is composed of two sides. Sometimes the other side is not clearly seen.

Intuition

Intuition does not explain. Intuition does not follow logic. Intuition does not always look reasonable. Intuition only points the way. Its whisper is soft. It says "that direction" or "this direction". Sometimes it is drowned out by the noise of daily life and the world-mind. In calm intuition can be heard just fine. Intuition sometimes makes suggestions that others wouldn't understand if you explain it to them.

Today I did not change the lanes on the Highway although someone was flashing his headlights for me to get out of the way so that he could pass. Normally I always make way. But not this time. I was asked: "Why don't you get out of the way? Someone wants to pass you!". This question was answered the very moment a car suddenly shifted from the 1st lane to the second...where I would have been had I switched. The accident would have been deadly. Looking that the car I responded: "That's why".

This happens all the time when you're in a calm state. You "just know". "Just Because".

True Power

For those in power to stay in power they must spread false information on how power is gained and maintained. The masses must be kept in darkness about how to increase their scope of influence and command in the world. They believe power is gained by money, greed, persuasion, domination, force – all of which are actually symptoms of *powerlessness*.

A few game rules of true power are shared within this article. In extrapolating these principles you will discover other things on your own.

Self-Importance vs. Others Importance

People are addicted to feeling important, special, better. You gain power not by Self-Importance, which makes you inert and manipulable, but by *making others important.* You are a unique individual. But by showing this too much and making yourself better than others, you will attract envy. People will want to put you down. By making *them* important, valuing *their* talents, beauty, achievements – you cater to their insecurity and needing of wanting to be better. Do not outshine your boss. You are not important. Your customers are. You are not important. Your superiors are. You are not important. Your colleagues are. You are not important. Others are. And as you give people what they long for, your own power increases.

Control of Others vs. Self Control

If you think trying to control others equals power you have been misinformed. Before seeking command over others, find *command of yourself.* You are all you truly have. The world and what you experience is a reflection of you. Control yourself and you control the world. In any situation where you are wanting to change others, have others think or feel something, manipulate others, you are in a state of lack. You cannot change others directly. In fact, if you attempt to do so, they will notice, and resist the change you seek in them even more. *Wanting* control equals *not having* control. If however, you are an example of poise, self-discipline and clarity, you will lead by that example. People will change in your presence not because you told them to change or tried to exert dominance over them, but because people always imitate the people who have the most energy. Others are a mirror. You cannot expect the mirror to change by demanding it to smile first.

Chatter vs. Silence

A lot of energy is wasted in mindless chatter, gossip, lying, not keeping your word and verbal focus on the unwanted and the unimportant. A lot of energy and power is accumulated in *Silence*. Insecure people can't stand silence and so they talk for the sake of talking – without purpose, reason or focus. But talking is creative, and when you are finished talking you have created a world from your words. Energy diffuses when your talking is pointless and unfocussed. "Where were you just now?" asks the wife. "I was taking the garbage out" answers the husband. And the point of this conversation? None.

Observe those who spend hours talking about the most mundane and unimportant things. Observe how they exhaust their energy, constantly focussing on issues that have nothing to do with their truest hearts desire. Lying and deception is another certain way to loose your power. How much creative power do you think your *Word* has if it turns out that that *Word* is untrue? Who will follow your command? Nobody. If you have spoken many things that did not come to fruition, your inner-self will take this is a signal that your word does not mean anything. Talking too much also overwhelms other peoples attention-spans with things they could not care less about. When you hold a speech in front of people, it is not only about what you say but also about what you do not say. Too much information will quickly bore them. Giving less information will keep them attentive. Say less than necessary. Never ever talk bad behind someone's back. Foul-mouthing others subtly reflects worse on yourself than on the person you are talking about.

Fixed Identity vs. Formlessness

Water resists nothing and nothing resists it. It is formless and easily passes through all situations. Having a fixed identity, fixed opinion, fixed lifestyle, fixed habits makes you predictable and easy to attack and break. Wood is easy to break. Water and Air are impossible to Break. Change is the only constant. Being thus always on the move or in a state of transformation, you cannot be located and fixed as a target. Do not succumb to the identities and roles society tries to bestow upon you. Be able and ready to adapt to different realities, countries, people, situations. Not being fixed in one position also allows you take on other peoples viewpoints – which, ultimately equals being able to lead them.

Reveal vs. Conceal

Do not reveal your goals, intentions, plans. Doing so will open them up to doubt and attack from others. But they cannot attack something they do not know about. They cannot doubt something they are unaware of. Revealing your goals before they are achieved can also stifle their very accomplishment. Never brag. Do not discuss your weaknesses in public or towards people you are not very close to. Remain elusive to the world. You need not justify every move you make. You need not report your location, whereabouts, past, present, future to the world. Remaining thus mysterious your appeal will grow.

Work vs. Productivity

Do not exhaust yourself with work you do not enjoy. If there is an important errand that must be done, do not procrastinate or postpone but get it over with quickly.

Spend the rest of your time doing things you enjoy. Allow your work to be creative and productive. Delegate the work you do not like to others or to "The Forces of the Universe". Money is not important. Approval from society is not important. Success is not important. These are superficial things. What is important is that you have joy in being productive and creative. In focussing purely on *creating value* for yourself and others, while ignoring all superficial desires, your power will increase. You will not catch many butterflies by hurriedly running through the field after them. Instead, use a bait that smells wonderful to butterflies and they will come to you – without much effort on your side. True Power gets more done with less effort.

Take vs. Give

Do not judge the day by what you reap but by what you sow. Ask not what you are getting, but what you can give. The beggar always seeks to receive, the wealthy man is always in a position to give. Instead of asking what a customer or a company or a group or society can do for you, ask what you can do for them.

Dishonesty vs. Integrity

In its original meaning the word "Integrity" means "Being part of the whole". This means to treat the world as you would like to be treated. If you manipulate others, you open yourself for being manipulated. Your inner power can create anything and everything – without needing to lie, steal or cheat. So remain clean. Maintain the highest standards of reputation and ethics you can. Then you will not have to feign or pretend to be in good standing (which costs a lot of energy). Keeping transgressions and evils secret sucks life energy out of you. It makes you vulnerable for attack. It makes you a target for blackmail. By obeying the ethics of your society and community you become someone who cannot be attacked or hurt. And if someone does decide to attack you or blame you for a wrong, it will reflect back on them – as no evidence of your wrong-doing can be found.

Reactive vs. Pro-Active or Non-Reactive

At the heart of powerlessness lies reactivity. Reacting to perceived enemies. Reacting to problems. Reacting to attacks. Whatever you react to, you assign importance and validity, thereby giving it power over you. When something you dislike happens: Either do not react to it at all, or become pro-active in the opposite direction.

The Forgiveness Technique

Feeling Resentment toward others does not hurt others it only hurts yo. The subconscious cannot tell the difference between resenting others and resenting yourself. It is therefore recommended that you release all types of Resentment. This technique is one way of doing it. Feel free to use your own Variations.

1. Write down the name of a person you would like to forgive.

2. Write down which thoughts and beliefs create the feeling of Resentment toward this person.

3. What problems must this person have had in order to behave that way? What do you assume are those persons feelings, thoughts and beliefs that compell him to behave in that way? And: If you were in the persons position, might you behave that way too? Write down your answers.

4. What negative energy came from you, prior to the other person doing that thing you havent forgiven? Can you see how you were Complaining, Blaming or in a bad

feeling space prior to that person?

5. If you pretend for a moment that its 10 years from now. Have you forgiven by now? How many years do you think is enough before you can forgive?

6. If you could forgive the person, how long would it take for that to feel natural?

7. If you could forgive the person, how would that make you feel?

8. Gently focus on yourself and the person. Ask yourself: Could I first forgive myself for resenting this person?

9. Focus on yourself and whisper: "I'm sorry. I forgive you. I love you."

10. Gently focus on yourself and the person. Ask yourself: Could I forgive this person?'

11. Gently focus on the person and ask yourself: Have I made similar mistakes before?

12- Gently focus on the person and ask yourself: When

could I forgive this person?

13. Focus on the person and whisper: "I'm sorry. I forgive you. Thank you."

Unlimited Being

Imagine a tiny dot on a white piece of paper. That tiny dot is what most people have narrowed their attention to and have identified with when thinking they are their body/mind. The rest of the piece of paper and beyond in all directions and dimensions is the vast expanse of all-that-is. Therefore, being more open in awareness rather than narrow and pinpointed goes more in the direction of that Unlimited Being and Cosmic Conciousness. Opening in this way, so that you are not only involved with the tiny dot but perhaps with at least the rest of the area surrounding that dot also allows you to more easily create new realities. Creating new realities would mean to create a new tiny dot. That is easier from a perspective outside the original dot. Otherwise you'd only be creating over the already existing dot…which would look messy.

So let's experience some of this Unlimited Being and not

only read about it. As you sit there, relax. Let go of any tension on the outbreathe. And as you sit there and read this, notice what you are aware of. You are aware of these words, but become aware of a little more. The sounds in your surroundings. What the chair you are sitting on feels like. Aware of your body. Aware of your breathing. Aware of the objects near you. You have now opened your awareness a little, expanded it from that tiny dot to something slightly bigger.

You are not that which you are aware of. Anything you can
observe you cannot at the same time *be*. You are not the cup, table, computer in your surroundings. As the observer, you are separate from them. Likewise you are not your body and mind. Don't take my word for it, check for yourself. Are you aware of your body as it is sitting there? Are you aware what you call "mind", that stream of thoughts coming and going?

Who is the one that's aware? You are identified with the body, obviously, and your awareness likes "hanging around" in or near the body and mind, but you are not that. Try pointing to where "me" resides. And if you now point to a part of your body, who is doing the pointing. The hand? Are you your hand? Not hardly. Your brain? Are you that piece of meat called brain? I doubt it. You are not a body or mind. If you are having a difficult time experiencing this right now, then could you at least acknowledge that your awareness is not limited to the body/mind?

Feel the Body. Now expand your attention to all the empty space surrounding your body. And expand your attention to some tree or object outside of the building you are in. You are experiencing that awareness/attention is not limited to the body. Otherwise all you could perceive is the body.

It is as simple as that. Many, when I speak of Unlimited Being and of experiencing that think they are going to skyrocket to a state of enlightenment. But experiencing Unlimited Being is more natural, more relaxed, more normal and also more attainable than that. You just did it. And rather than
going for the huge enlightenment I'd recommend you relax into what you already are and gradually deepen this small bit of relaxation you felt. You already are Infinite Being,
Unlimited Awareness, All-that-is. Actually there is

nothing to achieve, nowhere to go, nothing to do, no program to go through, nothing to solve. Beingness Just Is. The trees
just are. Your body and breathing just are. None of it requires your maintenance. None of it requires your extra effort. None of it requires your achievement. None of it needs to deserved. Feel that Beingness for a moment that is already whole and perfect, here, now.

If you could just sit still and aware and be present a few minutes a day you'd open a bit and rejuvenate because of that. What keeps you narrowly focussed on that small dot is
resistance toward what-is. And the only time we're willing to let go of all resistance and "Just Be", is during sleep. During sleep we allow ourselves to relax back into that vast expanse
which we are. And because of that we regenerate during sleep. So if you could do this for a few minutes while waking you would not need that much sleep and you'd also feel more refreshed throughout the day. *What-is* here and now requires no effort. So sit some minutes a day and just *Be*. Be that which is aware. Be that which is effortless and natural. And when you've accepted the state of being that has no resistances, no desires, no

needs, no urgencies, no obligations…then, if you still care, focus on the realities you prefer or do the jobs and activities you prefer.

10

How to Access Future Lives

The Technique for Accessing Future Lives is demonstrated on my Audio-Program "Journey to Another Life". You can use the same Technique but your Intention for using it should be on a Future-Self. I will give a written version of the Technique here. It uses the tool of Imagination to a collect information from otherwise hidden sources. This works best if you keep your Imagination disciplined and don't allow it to wander too much. "Keep with the Storyline" so to speak.

1. Intend

You intend that you would like to visit a Future Version of Yourself. You leave it up to your Higher Good which Future Life you will be shown.

2. Relax Deeply

You lie down and relax deeply. Give yourself at least 10 Minutes time to relax in your own way (music, breathing, yoga, just lying there, etc.).

3. Imagine Floating Upwards out of Body into Space

Imagine you leave your body. Imagine slowly and gradually floating up from your bedroom over your village and further up into space. Allow at least 3 to 5 Minutes for this transition. Your Imagination should be vivid and believable.

4. Imagine Floating Downwards into a New Body, a New Self

Give yourself 3 to 5 Minutes to gradually fall back down to the Planet, down into a new house, a new bed, a new body. Allow this other body to be whatever it is.

5. Open your eyes in the new Body and Explore

Allow yourself to feel your new body. In your Imagination, get up and explore your new body, your new surroundings and the new life you are in. Spend about 15 Minutes here. You can use music if you like (if you use music, prepare it prior to the Session. If you interrupt the Session to get up, you will have interrupted the ability to perceive properly. Imagination only gives you proper Information in a state of deep ease).

11

Soul Awakening Exercise

Complete this book by taking one of these wake-up-questions a day and considering it for that entire day. If it helps you remember, write down the question on a card and carry it around with you until you have practiced the idea or the idea it points to.

1. When was the last time I genuinely smiled?
2. When was the last time I genuinely laughed?
3. When was the last time I sang?
4. When was the last time I danced?
5. When was the last time told stories?
6. What value does my life have?
7. How can I be of service to the world?
8. If I lost my job, position, status, what meaning/value would my life still have?
9. What would I do if I loose everything?
10. What would I do if I already had everything?

11. What or who, if anything, would I die for?
12. What could I let go of because it no longer really serves me?
13. What has and has not worked last week?
14. What are my intentions for next week?
15. Where or with who could I practice being more loving and kind?

May the stars remind you of who you are...

Other Works by the Author

Frederick Dodson / Parallel Universes of Self (2007)

Frederick Dodson / Levels of Energy – Introduction to Spectral Consciousness (2009)

Frederick Dodson / The Reality Creation Technique (2010)

Frederick Dodson / Lives of the Soul (2010)

The Reality Creation Course (www.oceanofsilence.com)

Reality Creation Blog (www.realitycreation.org)

Reality Creation Audios (www.realitycreation.net)

You can contact the author at eternaloceanic@gmail.com

Printed in Great Britain
by Amazon